THE BIG DILEMMA

Do Life or Quit Life?

SOPHY CHUNGE

www.centfie.com

Dedication

To Gladys, Silas, and Haron, the family that is always there for me when I am not there for myself.

Acknowledgements

I thank everyone who helped in the creation of this book. Thanks to the clients and professionals who provided important information needed to prepare this book. Thanks to the psychological researchers who enhance our knowledge of mental health. I thank K. Joyce, O. Winnie, B. Michael, Antony, Eve, Musa, and all those who have shown me through action that true friendship exists. I appreciate all those who underestimate, despise and discourage me for their negativity is my fuel for success. Thanks for choosing to read this book.

ISBN: 978-9914-705-83-6

Contact

Phone: +254772625511
Email:sophychunge@gmail.com
          Kenya.

Disclaimer

This book is written for the sole purpose of creating mental health awareness. Any resemblance of the events and situations in this book to actual persons, living or dead, is coincidental. The content of this publication has been prepared based on psychological and counselling techniques. While the best efforts were utilised in the research and preparation of this book, the author does not make warranties with respect to the guidance and strategies contained herein. You may use the information herein at your own discretion. When necessary consult with a professional for appropriate diagnosis and therapy which is suitable for your personal situation. Neither the publisher nor the author shall be liable for commercial, incidental, consequential, or other damage.

"It is easy to tell the toiler
How best he can carry his pack
But no one can rate a burden's weight
Until it has been on his back."
—*Ella Wheeler Wilcox*

Contents

Dear fellow human being,

Thank you for picking this book *The Big Dilemma: Do Life or Quit Life?* It targets those tormented by thoughts of whether to end their life or to continue living. It will also be useful to the loved ones of someone who is facing "the big dilemma." This book is for the misunderstood, the misfits, and the heartbroken. It is a book about hope in struggle and victory in life.

The scope of *The Big Dilemma* covers the subject of capability for life and mental pain that leads to suicide. The premise of this book is based on the highly researched "Interpersonal Theory of Suicide."

Often, we give up in the face of adversity despite having the potential to live. It breaks my heart every time I hear someone has ended their own life. It hurts me more when people kill themselves because of a similar set of circumstances which I have gone through and managed to come out victorious despite losing hope at some point. Others who are in a similar situation can realise that they can make it too.

Consider this an informative book. Anyone can learn and gain something, but you have to make your own choice concerning practical application. You can take what suits you and leave what doesn't.

The Big Dilemma uses a psychotherapeutic approach and not an advice-giving approach. It is meant to facilitate coping, decision-making, and problem-solving skills. It can only provide you with tips. At no point should it replace the services of mental health professionals.

The capability for life is already in you. This book is a tool meant to remind you of your capability to live. I hope that you are willing to receive encouragement and that you will enhance your resilience. May you be inspired, soothed, and encouraged!

The Big Dilemma is a suicide prevention tool dedicated to humanity. It applies researched-based techniques in a simplified way so that you do not have to read research papers or get a PhD in human psychology.

Read through the book, try out the tips outlined, carry out the suggested activities and examine the results. This is one way of saying "You are not alone in this. You can get through this. You can still live despite the challenges you face." Whatever you do, as long as you keep your life and you do not harm other people's lives, keep doing it. You can handle your problems while living.

Personal circumstances vary. Individual experiences account for the different personal perspectives on life, the world, and society.

Everyone has their unique perception of their experiences with life which differ from many others. Therefore, no other human being has the power to force you to handle your problems in a certain way. You can maintain your freedom of mind even when you are physically or socially bound. *The Big Dilemma* does not claim to have all the answers for your spiritual or philosophical questions about life.

It is acceptable to disagree when you deem some techniques herein unfit for your personal situation. However, the preservation of life, especially human life, is universally accepted and pursued. Which life are you best equipped to preserve as much as possible?

We are all equal by virtue of BEING here in existence on planet Earth. This is certain: there are others before us, and others are coming after us who will face the same dilemma. We can learn from those who have been through it and fought the battle of life to the end without quitting out of their own volition. Are you humble enough to listen to others despite their different points of view if they support a pro-life choice?

Whether you are experiencing mental pain due to a momentary problem or physical illness, do life. Whether you are coerced or manipulated into quitting life, keep living. Acknowledge your presence. Appreciate your ability to breathe. Accept the being part of "human being."

May you be motivated to make a habit of understanding your mental aches and coping with them rather than letting them curb your desire to live. This book will not solve your problems. You can choose to solve your problems by applying the suggested principles to see if they work for you.

Regarding your passion for life, encourage and nourish it. This book can help you nurture, reward or celebrate it. It cannot instil in you a passion for life and uninstall a passion to quit. A book can't make it grow, but you can do what needs to be done to make your life liveable.

Remember, your own life is the greatest project to work on. As long as you are alive, make it worth your while. Treat your life as a unique privilege. It does not deserve to be ended by your inclination. Do life. Don't quit. Today is the day, now is the time to embark on this project called life.

May you be motivated to keep living, give an inspirational talk, start a mental health organization, or join in the collective effort to encourage our fellow human beings to "do life" and to continue being. Better yet, you might even write a critique of this book.

Although circumstances are propelling you to quit life, keep reading. Give this material a chance to speak to you. Put aside your biases and stereotypes and read on.

You might find tips to help yourself or someone else. This book does not claim to have the life-changing secret to happiness and bliss forever. It is designed to point you in the direction of choosing to live. It is not meant to fix or correct you. Possibly some of the proven psychological techniques used herein require improvement. I welcome criticism, feedback and suggestions.

If *The Big Dilemma* touches one person's heart and inspires one person to keep living, I will count that as an enormous success. This is my way of taking part in mental health awareness campaigns. I hope my words will exhort you to safeguard your life diligently.

Thank you for choosing to read *The Big Dilemma: Do Life or Quit Life?* We most likely don't know each other, but I am with you in living. Let's do it!

S.C 2019

Chapter 1: The Dilemma

Live it or leave it? Do it or quit it? You might be stuck in this dilemma about your life. You are considering suicide as a way out of your distress. Life has come to a dead-end where you feel like it is unbearable. Or you deem the future full of suffering which you cannot withstand.

Congratulations! For when your life becomes harder and you go on undeterred, you have the chance to become stronger.

When you get through tough times, you will become tougher. The more you go through challenging times, the higher your chances of hardening. With this hardening comes self-advancement and progress. Now that you are not dead yet, you have the capability for survival.

To illustrate, think of computer games that have levels which the user has to surpass—like the reputable *Candy Crush Saga*. You will not level up unless you go through challenge after challenge and overcome them.

A quitting habit gets you stuck in one level. The more you grow, the more the hardships experienced and the more you need to think about your next step before taking it.

As much as you are thinking of ending it all, it is likely that you feel afraid of yourself. You have become a threat to yourself, and you know it alright although you desire to keep living.

Take steps to safeguard your life when plagued with suicidal ideation. Live on. Do not allow the disappointments of momentary losses that can heal with time, to make your mind perceive the world as unbearable. The livableness of your life is intact.

By virtue of being a human being, you can overcome temporary and permanent losses and triumph over the disappointments, suffering and pain that you experience in this world.

This requires seeking the help of the One who created us and He puts other people in place to assist us. It is your choice to accept the help available to you.

Human beings from all walks of life are faced with this big dilemma—should I do life or quit life? They get stuck between choosing whether to do life or to quit life often trapped hopelessly in misery and unhappiness.

Unfortunately, privilege, social status, financial success, and academic prowess do not exempt you from feeling like you have to quit living.

A quitting habit, accompanied by psychological pain, has pushed accomplished people who seemed to be passionate about life with a bright future ahead of them to quit life.

Smart people from different professional backgrounds such as doctors, engineers, teachers, and lawyers have quit. Talented people such as chefs, designers, musicians, and artists have quit. The unemployed, the homeless, and the sufferers who have trouble getting a meal on the table have given up on themselves and quit.

The thought of quitting life besets many of us, and most of us choose life. Although it can be tough, we stand tougher.

You can join this universal will to live. Though your life is tough, seize every tough experience as an opportunity for advancement. Your life is your first teacher. How you live it will give you lessons for future reference.

After all, life ends in death after which you can do nothing. Do life while you still can. Don't give up the struggle to turn your life around. Getting unstuck from a quitting mentality is usually difficult in the beginning.

Take an honest self-examination of yourself. Do you get defensive when well-meaning people try to comfort you during obviously difficult times?

Do you always consider yourself right and others wrong? Do you have trouble letting go of old habits which you know are causing problems in your life?

Open yourself to new perspectives and lessons rather than doing things the way you have always done.

If one way is not working, you have to look for an alternative way. Note that, you need to be alive to take that other way. You don't have to quit life. When you are busy rebelling and fighting against life, it might look harder than it is. Often, you have to flow with life, adapt to change and embrace change.

If you can answer "I am willing" to some of these questions, then you have no business quitting life, you have so much to live for, and you are going to live and never kill any human being. You will not kill yourself. You will live.

- Are you willing to get another perspective to life which directs you to continue to live?
- Are you willing to give up perceptions, limiting beliefs and habits which are worsening your predicament?
- Are you willing to seek help even though you believe that you are being misunderstood?
- Are you willing to select the growth choice over the cessation choice?

You are a singular, unique being though you identify with mankind as a whole. Every one of us can be affected by this dilemma—should I do life or quit life? Remember, in life and death human beings are equal. If other human beings can continue to live despite extremely painful conditions or situations, so can you.

The individual human life comprises of some of the highest moments of happiness and the lowest moments of sadness. You can take charge of your own life and choose to live in a way that will increase your prospects for happiness. Say yes to life. Repaint your life even when the colours wash away. Instead of quitting you can do life and strive to improve your individual experience of the world. Make a pact with yourself. Make an agreement with yourself. You will keep living. You are willing to live.

It is hard to encourage yourself to live if you can't define life.

What is life? Complete the following sentences:
1. Life is a.....................
2. Life is the.................
3. Life is.......................

Defining "doing life."

Before we get into the tough job of considering other alternatives to suicide which are protective of life, let's get a brief overview about what it means to "do life" or "quit life" in the context of this book.

The word "do" has many formal and informal meanings and can be used in many ways including derogatory. What comes to your mind when you read the phrase "do life?" In this book, "do" is used in contrast to "quit."

Doing life means performing the actions involved in living. We could say live life, but that is more specific and a bit limiting. To do life is a deliberate act of taking action that preserves your life. It involves working on your life, caring for your life and keeping your life in order.

Defining "quitting life."

Quitting is the deliberate act of ending something. You can quit a job, a relationship, or a harmful habit. Thus, quitting is not always a bad thing. However, quitting life is the deliberate ending of one's life. It is often a result of a previous pattern of quitting when the going gets tough.

Ending the life of a human being is universally considered to be an act of violence. Therefore, killing oneself is a fatal act of violence toward oneself. Often, violence is triggered by intensified emotions such as anger, grief and shame. Suicide might be an expression of anger toward oneself or another person. Suicide is fatal, some people survive it some do not. Individual reasons account for the motivation to either do life or quit life.

Risk factors for suicide

Researchers in the field of human behaviour have a hard time finding subjects to study for suicide because most of the victims are not here.

However, they have identified some of the predisposing factors for suicidal thinking and behaviour. These stressors can increase an individual's desire to commit suicide.

Not all people on earth who go through these situations, outlined in the following list, end up quitting life. Some people experience the direst of situations without losing their motivation to live. On the other hand, others face what most people would consider a tiny problem, but to them, it is big enough to trigger suicidal thinking.

These stressors usually affect the quality of individual life so much that life becomes intolerable. Thus, you consider suicide as a logical way to end your suffering. Check out the following list and see if you identify with some of these stressors in your life.

1. Psychosocial factors
   - unemployment
   - societal stigma
   - significant economic changes
   - social status changes
   - religious beliefs
   - incarceration
   - guilt and shame
   - alcohol/drug intoxication

2. Individual psychological vulnerabilities
   - impulsiveness
   - unhappiness
   - hopelessness
   - anxiety
   - self-consciousness
   - social disengagement
   - aggression
   - failure

3. Psychiatric disorders
   - Major Depressive Disorder (depression)
   - Bipolar Disorder
   - Schizophrenia
   - Anxiety Disorders

- Eating Disorders
- Attention Deficit Hyperactivity Disorder
- Substance Use Disorders
- Personality Disorders e.g. Borderline Personality Disorder

4. History of traumatic events
- physical abuse
- sexual abuse
- emotional abuse
- disasters
- grief and loss
- domestic violence
- past suicide attempts
- family history of suicide
- self-harming behaviours
- divorce
5. Physical pain
- terminal illnesses
- functional bodily impairments
- disfigurement
- increased dependence on others
- chronic pain

Possible solutions

This is a list of 10 mitigating factors which can reduce an individual's risk of suicidal behaviour. This book focuses on refining these areas. Therefore, keep these items in mind as you read.

1. Strong social support networks including family and friends
2. Good problem-solving ability
3. Cultural and religious beliefs which oppose suicide
4. Responsibility to others
5. Seeking help from support networks and mental health practitioners
6. Openness to new experiences in life
7. Goal-setting and making plans
8. Increasing tolerance to distress
9. Improving coping skills
10. Increasing self-esteem

Chapter 2: *Psychache*

This book focuses on the most common issue that troubles us when we contemplate suicide. That is, the pain inside that makes life unbearable and all prospects dim.

The thought to quit life usually has an internal rather than an external source. External sources are often motivators of the internal thought processes. The psychological pain might have a lot of sources including physical causes like terminal illnesses or chronic physical pain. The cause for the psychological pain might differ, but the effect is the same.

Researchers have found that mental pain, also referred to as *Psychache*, contributes to suicidal thinking and behaviour. Frequent painful circumstances or trauma can cloud your judgment and make it seem like life is an enemy.

Psychological pain is a great neutralizer. In the face of mental pain, all the things we use as a yardstick for measuring our differences fall away. It does not discriminate by race, gender, ethnicity, occupation, social status, economic status, cadre, religion or any other dividing factor. You are not exempted from mental pain just because you are a wealthy and successful person.

Human minds are made similarly just as human bodies are structurally the same. The internal workings of our bodies and mind are alike. Our way of natural breathing is the same. We all suffer at some point in our lives and we all die. All that matters is—can you breathe now?

Many people who face extreme mental pain think of quitting life. You do not want to kill yourself, but you knowingly put yourself in danger hoping someone else will kill you. You want to die, and since suicide itself takes courage, you want to be killed so that this pain can end.

The desire can be so intense that you don't consider you do not want life to end. You want the unfavourable situation, the pain and the suffering, to end.

Intense mental pain can blind you to other ways of reducing your uncomfortable situation to manageable levels. You see suicide as the only way to escape or end it. Yet, some types of pain can be done away with completely by changing your mindset and your interpretations of the circumstances.

Unlike physical pain, psychological pain cannot be handled with pain relief medications. Psychoactive medication can alter with your brain chemistry to adjust the state of consciousness and give you an impression of feeling good.

But, since the effects are often short-lived, such chemical substances can result in addictive behaviour to keep numbing the *Psychache*. Gradually, people who engage in addictive behaviours to numb their mental pain succumb to suicide because the addiction is just a cover-up and not a solution. You can find a better solution as long as you are alive.

However, not everyone who experiences extreme psychological pain thinks of suicide. Not everyone who contemplates suicide commits suicide. How do other people manage to continue living despite the psychological pain? This book will outline some psychological and critical thinking tips you can use to manage *Psychache*. May you find what works for you!

Identifying *Psychache*

Note which negative emotions you have experienced in your life.

- Hopelessness
- Guilt
- Grief
- Loneliness
- Worthlessness
- Regret
- Anxiety
- Fear
- Shame

- Rejection
- Unhappiness
- Frustration
- Helplessness
- Anger

Which emotion are you feeling now to the most degree? Which of these do you often feel?

Dissect that painful emotion. This can help with conquering the actual problem. Delve down into your ache, penetrate through it rather than seeking immediate relief. Get to the core of the pain. Understand why you feel the way you do. Feel the feeling first. Don't repress it.

Can you change the situation? Is the situation beyond your control (e.g. controlled by nature, other people) or is it within your power?

Then, think about:
1. What do you gain from holding on to *psychache?*
2. What can you do to lessen *psychache?*
3. What is within your power to do about the cause of the *psychache?*

Fear and pain

Fear and pain make you vulnerable to *Psychache*. The fear of the future and what it holds for you breeds hopelessness. Yet, some kinds of pains are temporary. Just because it is distressing you now does not mean it will last forever. You can conquer the fear of the unknown future and the fear of suffering. You can conquer the fear of societal stigma. It is normal to be afraid of being ashamed or guilty because you have made mistakes. Your mistakes don't have to be the end of the world for you. You can rectify.

Even if you anticipate to be ashamed and you can't bear it, shame does not last. People will talk, they will criticise and judge you but when they face similar situations or worse, they will forget. Learn to ignore most of what society thinks. Your life is too big a price to pay for society's disapproval.

Physical pain especially prolonged pain due to illness or injury can become so extreme that all you desire is death. In certain occasions, where it is legal, doctors opt for euthanasia. However, so many people have overcome the worst pain imaginable and lived to inspire others. If your illness has not killed you yet, if you can manage the pain, will yourself to endure. Being alive is a privilege. Consider how others try their best to save their lives. Your presence is important.

Ask anyone who has had their loved one in a coma or critically ill for a long time. You'd think since they expected death, it wouldn't hurt very much. But, when death takes them away, they feel extreme grief. Their presence mattered a lot, even though they were in a useless state. As long as you have life and you can breathe, there is always hope. Your presence matters.

You can deal with and overcome most things you set your mind to. Seek help from mental health professionals if you can afford. If not, talk to someone willing to listen. Call the hotlines available in your country. Always seek help when you are going through a mental breakdown.

With appropriate help, you can overcome or at least lessen guilt, heartbreak, loneliness, regret, grief and all kinds of mental pain. These negative emotions do not mean life is pointless.

Managing your fears and pains is the first step of thwarting the thoughts and plans of ending your life. You can succeed in staying alive despite the external causes of suffering. You can get help from friends, family, and even strangers as long as you do not die in silence or fear people's perception of you.

Understanding *Psychache*

Negative emotions will pass if you let them pass. Holding on to them gets you attached to pain. Psychological pain does not trap and cage you, you trap and cage it. You might encounter it again and again, but if you learn to let it go it will go. When you hold on, it will hold on to you in return. If you release it, it will release its hold on you. Cry, scream, write, sing, make art and let it out constructively and harmlessly. Feel the pain when it comes, but don't hold on to it. Let it go on its way. Let it pass because, sadly, in due time another pain will come your way.

Life has often been compared to a road trip. Picture this; you are on a highway. You often encounter other people on the same route you are taking. Their means might be similar or different from yours. On this road of life, some people will overtake you. Don't quit because your pace seems slower than others'. Don't lose patience.

Sometimes you may get the privilege of flying rather than using the road. Sometimes there are storms and you need to rest for a while and let them pass. Sometimes resting during the storm is not an option and you have to negotiate through it. In this journey, the solution is to always move forward because, in the end, the experience gives life its importance.

In life, you will encounter different states of mind like happiness, sadness and other emotions along the way. Drive, ride or walk, comfortably, do not try to overtake pain and avoid it, you have to pass through it. Some obstacles are a mirage and you need to get close to recognize the illusion. Slow down and climb over the bump, instead of getting angry at the existence of the bump. No amount of anger about the bump will make it disappear. Although the bump may appear to be a mountain when you are worn-out and in pain, it is still just a bump.

At times you simply need to be patient until the fog clears. The fog threatens to control your journey. It blinds you to other prospects of the journey. Don't allow yourself to be defined by the fog. You have to persevere through the fog because there is no other way around it, there's no shortcut, but through it. Your view of life is clouded by a dense fog of pain, but the other path might just be around the corner. Move on and get on with living.

Life is sometimes easy and effortless, but sometimes it is difficult and demanding. It differs across different phases of your life. You will not always be on the same flat road all through, sometimes you will encounter unfavourable weather, roadblocks, unexpected potholes, uphill climbs and downhill descents, dangerous bridges where you are hanging on a balance, or good bridges where you drive through without worry.

Never-ending psychological pain can make it seem like you have no moment of ease and your journey is all about climbing uphill.

Help-seeking and Coping with *Psychache*

Some pains are momentary, they do not put a dense fog over you. However, at some point during the journey, you might need headlights or torches to guide your way. When it is too hard to go on, fellow travellers on this journey can point you in the right direction. Either they have experienced that route you are on, or they have studied their journey through and through.

Be unafraid to seek help when you need it. They might not solve your problem, because it takes your inner will to do that, but they might help lessen your burden. In case someone points out to you that there is danger ahead on the road you are taking, and they try to assist, kill the ego and take a moment to open yourself up to assistance.

Sometimes you need to reach out for help instead of expecting the other travellers to automatically identify your needs and offer help. Remember their means is not always the same as yours and their starting point is probably your destination or vice versa.

We do not choose the stations that we find ourselves in when we begin to live. Hence, even though they are on the same road, they might be unable to understand your challenges.

Sometimes you need help because the fog has covered your vision perhaps due to an overwhelming burden of negative emotions. Sometimes you need help to offload. Always seek help, regardless of how embarrassed or vulnerable you might feel. Unwillingness to receive help might cost you your life by making the load more unbearable.

You have the responsibility to live your life. Seeking assistance might be the antidote to your thoughts of quitting.

Who can help you? God, spiritual mentors, psychotherapists, counsellors, trusted friends or family members or strangers who identify with your plight.

It is not easy to trust others when you have experienced betrayal after trusting people before. This is one reason why counselling can be an ideal way to explore your feelings authentically, honestly, deeply, and without fear.
The ideal counselling relationship is a safe place to reprogram yourself. The counsellor is restricted by professional ethics. So, the chances of breaching your trust are minimal.

Unfortunately, not all your efforts to seek help will be successful because other people do not identify with your situation or they are too busy trying to cope with their personal problems.

This is no reason to give up. When you realize that other people cannot help you, it is upon you to decide not to quit seeking. There is always someone who is willing to help.

Furthermore, being patient helps. Also, there is always someone you can help. When you help others instead of only expecting help, your vision will clear and you will discover you can manage the situation on your own after all.

Despite everything, life is fine, life is beautiful, life is good, and life is okay. The pain clouds your perception. Stressful personal circumstances mess with your vision. In the darkness, the harmless tree shrub will appear to be a terrifying monster.

We often need guidance through the fog and darkness, but guidance will only work if we are willing to listen and apply it. Be willing to accept assistance from the right places. Not everyone cares, but some do.

Chapter 3: The Aridity of Life

The experience of the aridity of life goes beyond ethnicity, race, social status, economic status, religious affiliation, and gender. Aridity is the state of not yielding anything of value, lacking interesting values, or lacking success. Without the fulfilment of spiritual and psychological needs, the aridity of life is overwhelming.

See the following. Check on which you agree. Does your life ever feel this way? Kindly be honest with yourself.

- Fatiguing
- Boring
- Uninspiring
- Useless
- Shameful
- Humiliating
- Hopeless
- Unsuccessful

Individual lives consist of experiences that require a good deal of sweat. They can be exhausting to both the mind and the body. In the scope of general human experience, "arid" experiences of life are usual. There's nothing strange or new about low moments.

It does not matter what kind of background you have—whether you are less known or well known, or whether you are spoilt for car choice or you have nothing to your name.

The aridity of life is a representative phenomenon, but not everyone experiences it in the same way since the quantity of aridity differs from one person to another. For others, it is the first experience while it is a frequent experience for some.

For others, it is all they have known throughout their lives and the aridity is normal life to them.

In the same way, not everyone who contemplates suicide quits life. Some contemplate suicide, but they adjust their mindset and their suicidal thoughts are replaced with pro-life thoughts. This might be a result of support from significant others, lessons learnt, improved circumstances, or experiences which change their viewpoint.

Some fight suicidal thoughts daily. Thus, their purpose in life becomes fighting suicidal thoughts. Every day they live becomes an achievement in their personal quota of life.

Find Your Oasis

Does your life ever feel this way? Kindly be honest with yourself. Very honest. Dig deep and you shall find. Even if it was a brief moment of this.

- Relaxing
- Cheerful/Exciting
- Interesting
- Enriching
- Inspiring
- Joyful
- Hopeful
- Successful

Individual life also consists of experiences which feel good to both the mind and body. In the scope of general human experience, "fruitful" experiences of life are usual. There's nothing strange or new about wonderful moments.

Your oasis is inner happiness and the source of your true relief. Strive to be happy. If happiness was easy to achieve, life would not have a purpose. You sure desire a perfect world where you are happy all the time.

But, at the moment, there is nothing like that. You have to bear with the aridity while searching for the oasis.

You have to bear with the bad situations that beset you while living. You can find your purpose by striving against the odds and have both dreams and broken dreams. Yes, one dream is not enough.

Through life's journey, you will go through deserts where you may feel like you are all alone and your chances of survival seem pretty slim because you cannot sustain yourself, and it seems there is no one around to offer assistance. Thing is, you are never alone in the desert.

Somehow life is the struggle all of us have. You have to struggle to maintain your own life for your own sake and that of others who might depend on you. You are someone else's oasis, and quitting will worsen the aridity of their lives. Despite the harshness of life, you can prevail if you keep searching until you find your oasis.

Human beings have a spiritual need that can only be filled by The One who made us. That's where you will find the source of your oasis, which will replenish you during periods of aridity.

Love, Faith and Hope

"No one loves me."
"No one can ever love me."
"I am unlovable."

Sentiments like these foster hopelessness and lack of faith. Other people enjoy life and live it live despite unfortunate circumstances maybe poverty, while others do not enjoy their lives despite having enormous financial success, power, and fame.

In due course, you will learn that there is a void material things cannot fill. A spiritual void that requires filling with intangible aspects namely love, faith, and hope. Find love, faith, and hope and there you have your oasis. With these, you will find peace and freedom.

Life without love is a typical example of the aridity of life. Love is like the moisture that waters our personal lives.
Love is what drives most people toward great success. Love for yourself and others conquers fruitless thoughts. You are alive and you can love yourself for who you are.

Remember, your mind recalls and stores what you tell it the most, so frequently tell your mind what you want it to believe. Instead of complaining about how the situation is, rise to the occasion and take steps to make the situation be what you would like it to be.

This is what hope means. Being so grateful for possessing the ability to live that you can conceptualize good results despite knowing negative outcomes might be experienced. Focus your thoughts on what you are grateful for in life.

Minimize your focus toward the negativity in life or conceptualizing of bad results only. You can live despite everything else.

Some homeless persons, orphans, refugees and survivors of tragic happenings would rather just end it, but they keep living despite their terrible circumstances because the presence of life gives them hope. Living is something they can do well. It only requires breath, the ability to breathe and a way to earn a living.

You make the mind used to a certain way of thinking, you will always perceive the world according to your negative mindset. (See Chapter 14.)

A constantly negative mind will always notice the aridity of life whilst missing the oasis when it is right ahead. Choose a loving, hopeful, and faithful mindset. Be grateful for life itself. Living is a privilege to be treasured.

Loving to Live

People who love to live, do not try to escape the aridity of their personal lives. Instead, they face it and seek creative ways to deal with the arid situation.

When they find their oasis they utilize it to the best of their ability and save some water for future use because the lesson they have learnt is that it takes a while to find your oasis. It may seem hopeless, yet the oasis is just around the corner.

Deal with life as it comes enjoying the ups and using the downs as a test of your grit. Allowing them to mould you into the stronger person you desire to be. You will experience numerous challenges in your life and sometimes it will seem like the overall trend is toward unlimited suffering.

Decide today that when difficult times come you will remind yourself there is more to life than suffering and despair.

And the things that may appear little and insignificant in life might just be the things that never lose their value despite what you are going through. Such as the value of your heartbeat, your metabolism, and breathing mechanism.

Find out how to expose the importance of other things in life you are probably taking for granted.

Appreciate your life. Loving to live means acceptance of life as it is. Some days are bad, some days are good. Hardships nurture your strength of spirit and mind. Misfortunes will make you lose your footing, stagger or fall, but you will develop the strength of mind needed to continue to do life.

Chapter 4: Commitment to Live

What is your current life plan? Is it wise to have a life plan and yet life is fragile? We know for sure that life is unpredictable. So, what is the point of setting up a plan for your life? Why plan when unforeseen events that disrupt your plans happen all the time?

You can't control the whole future of humanity, and things might go against your plans. The worst thing that can get in the way of your life plans is death. Meanwhile, you can make your existence meaningful while you are still alive by setting goals and taking necessary action to achieve them.

What is the difference between people who love to live and people who hate their own lives so much that they want to quit? How come some human beings lack enthusiasm for life and all that can be done with life, yet others have so much enthusiasm toward life?

People who love life have a commitment to live. They have plans and goals they can only achieve if they are alive. They go to great lengths to seek ways of prolonging their lives. Armed with plans and plans after failed plans, they have a purpose to live because they look ahead to the future with the hope of achieving it.

They understand how fragile life is, and they want to use their lifetime efficiently.

You can reach such a level of loving life too. By looking at your present moment, living now, but thinking optimistically about the future. You will be strong, things will work out for you and life will be bearable.

Having a plan helps you to know your current position. You get something to stand for at the present moment. It is tough to get out of a disempowered mode.

Having plans and acting on them can ignite the desire to keep looking forward to their accomplishment. Plans will help you to take charge of your actions rather than relying on other people to drive your life for you.

Have plans for your life. Spontaneous living is great, but planning for the priority things in your life leads to satisfaction when you achieve the results.

A life plan can lower your chances of losing direction. A life plan increases your chances of finding meaning in your life. When you have a life plan, you have something to live for.

Things to Remember When Making Life Plans

Be flexible
Remember there is no perfect life plan. You may plan for your life perfectly, but things have a way of not always going the way we want them to.
Thinking about that does not make you a pessimist, it makes you sensible. Be flexible in case your life plan is disrupted. Otherwise, a slight disruption of your plans might become the end of your life.

While having a life plan is important, flexibility and adaptability is a required skill. You don't have to choose suicide. You can choose to adapt and reset your goals.

Be reasonable
Make reasonable plans based on what you can control to a certain level at least. For example, a plan of marrying at a certain age is beyond your control because someone else is involved.
Unless you have similar life plans, it is unwise to force other people to fit into your plans. Also, you cannot plan for everything. Life is sweet with some spontaneity in it. Have fun sometimes. Enjoy as long as you don't lose focus.

Be ready for challenges
Remember you will face obstacles. No one lives a life without challenges. The type or intensity of challenges may differ from person to person, but there is no escaping them.

Therefore, while making life plans, prepare for challenges. If possible, consider a get-a-way plan or a solution to those potential problems. When life has other plans that threaten your original plan, surf with it by reviewing your plans as you go on.

Be your own hero
Circumstances and privileges in individual life differ from one person to another. In the course of pursuing your plans, enjoy your achievements measured against yourself.

Avoid unreasonable comparisons to another person or your perception of another person's suffering or success.

Do You Have a Plan for Quitting Life?

Let's assess the extent of your plans for quitting. When you experience suicidal thinking how long does the urge last? Do you think you have the courage to quit or are you afraid to act? Do you already have a plan of how you are going to quit life?

Before you quit, remember, you are still alive. That water will continue flowing, that rope, pill, knife, gun —those are dead things. You are like a river. Sometimes you may feel dead inside, but there's so much life in you. Every breath you take is a manifestation of the existence of your life.

If you have not reached the stage where you have come up with ways of quitting life, you can prevent yourself from reaching there. If you already have thought and planned how to kill yourself, counter this by planning with the same zeal on how to stay alive.

Checklist: Strategic Plan for Living

Companies usually come up with strategic plans for their perceived success. A company which crops up without careful consideration is likely to fail. Most founders, therefore, usually set up teams to come up with a strategic goal.

They deliberate on the actions they need to take to achieve their goals based on their vision. The same can be applied to your life.

You must be alive to work toward your goals.

Your life is more precious than any business on earth because no one can replace you. Businesses can be easily copied and revived by other people. Since your life is precious, don't you need to have a strategic plan for this life?

Your life is the greatest project you can work on.

It can be difficult to choose where to start your life planning. We will not use specific details because you know your circumstances better. We are going to look at a simple guide based on the basic principles of strategic planning. Try applying them in your life. For a more personalized plan, please see a counsellor or mentor.

The following checklist can guide you on life planning.

1.   Vision

Have a vision. Set your goals in life. Break them down into various parts of your life.

Have a vision for every area of your life such as academics, career, finances, relationships, spirituality, and the like. Your vision will keep you from engaging in distractions which do not add value to your life. What would you like to see in your future self?

2.   Goals

You have a goal, but to reach the main goal in life you have to set up smaller goals. What do you want to achieve in the short-term and the long-term respectively? Set life goals with the assumption that you will live as long as possible.

However, in my opinion, time frames should be set for short-term goals, say, within five years. Choose goals which will enhance your life at the present moment. What would you like to achieve the most?

3. Action plan

Create your life's action plan. Outline plans for achieving your goals and the actions required to achieve them. Think about what you should do and what you should not do.

Consider things in your life that could hinder you from reaching your goals and cut them off. Maximize on the actions that will lead you toward your vision. What actions will lead you toward achieving your goals?

4. Learning

Learning is the way to grow. Generally, learning involves reading, listening, and experimenting.

Seek training to gain the knowledge and skills needed to achieve your goals. You may find a mentor to guide you. Read books or study to expand your knowledge.

What do you understand about life, living and yourself? Some lessons about life can only be learned through experience. Keep the lessons you learn from experience in mind when making your life plan.

Pursue personal, professional, or spiritual growth. Keep developing yourself, your relationships, your career, your businesses and your life. What do you need for improvement? How can you move to the next level?

5. Contingency plan

Have a life contingency plan. Identify the weaknesses you have and come up with measures of overcoming them. Think about the likely challenges you might face in life and the possible solutions. For example, people plan for emergencies by setting aside some funds and people plan for their loved ones by writing wills or getting life insurance coverage.

Make required adjustments when unanticipated events get in the way. Life seems unmanageable when a twist of events messes with your plans. You can choose to get stuck in the miserable debris of failed plans or get up and try again.

6.   Plan execution

After planning for your life what next? Coming up with your life plan is the easy part. The main challenge is taking action. Putting your plan into action calls for practising self-discipline and mental strength.

Since it is your life, no one can push you to follow your plan. You might have the best plan ever for a successful life, but if you do not implement the required actions, your chances of achievement decrease.

Summary
What are your plans in life and how far ahead have you planned? If you haven't yet, start now. If you have already made plans, aspire to follow them. In case it is not working, review your plans to fit your current circumstances. Make your life better by strategic life planning and taking action.

Chapter 5: Self-love and Self-acceptance

Many people have stereotypes about who you are. They have this idea of the person they believe you to be, and they believe they are right. They never see beyond the concrete wall they have built to define you.

Have you confined yourself into the same limited definition of yourself? You always know yourself better than other people do. Possibly, you have stereotypes about people, and you refuse to see beyond what you believe they are. If you can't see the good in yourself, how can you genuinely appreciate the good in others without envy and jealousy?

Without self-love and self-acceptance, you'll find it hard to do life. Self-love and self-acceptance begin with loving and accepting your life as it is, and yourself as you are. Loving and accepting your life means:

- You support yourself instead of self-sabotaging.
- You are strong and powerful even when you fail.
- You give yourself more positive than negative messages.
- You trust yourself to do everything for the best interest of your life.

Self-love

Do you love and accept yourself? Love yourself, as no one can love you better than you can love yourself. The first step to loving you is to know who you are. Eliminate the stereotypes you hold about yourself and other people. Define yourself when all other external views are not included.

- Who are you? You are what you do. If you help someone today, you are a hero. If you try to do something different today, you are creative.
- What can you do? You can live and the rest will follow. Remember your abilities, talents, and skills are only useful when you are alive.

In order to love yourself more, ask yourself how you can make your personal life experiences better. Not in competition with another person, but measured by where you are now. Consider what you want to change about your life and what you can do to cause it to happen.

Actions that can help you to keep loving yourself (you can add more.)

1. Helping other people when it is within your ability to do so.
2. Spending more of your time with people who believe in you.

3. Accepting both your flaws and strengths.

4. Learning to say no and putting yourself first when it doesn't harm anyone.

5. Sticking to your good habits and quitting the harmful ones.

6. Engaging in fun activities and hobbies.

7. Taking care of your physical, mental, and spiritual well-being.

8. Asking for and accepting help when you need it.

What qualities would you like in someone you love? To love yourself, nurture qualities which you would like someone you love to have. Give yourself the love you give to another. Give yourself the love you seek from other people. Love yourself the way you want to be loved by others. Treat yourself as you want someone who you love to treat you. Give yourself some dose of loyalty and honesty as you expect from the one you love. Every day greet your reflection with a smile and hug yourself.

Love yourself so much that your happiness does not rely on other people's perception of you. How can you complain that no one loves you when you are living and capable of loving yourself? You are not, "no one."

Buyers usually set their preferred prices of their goods. In the same way, set your value at priceless and accept it at that. Your life is not preserved for another person to love. Your life is yours to love. You can't love yourself without loving life. You can't love your life without loving yourself.

Self-acceptance

It is unfortunate when you downgrade yourself until you do not see your worthiness. Life loses its meaning when you spend it demeaning yourself to the point where you think you are useless. No one can love you better than you can love yourself.

Stop treating yourself as an inanimate thing that can only be loved by others. By virtue of being a human being, you have the capability to love and accept yourself.

You have control over your self-love and self-acceptance. Do what you can, leave what you can't control. You have no power over people's love, acceptance or regard of you.
Other people are also fighting their own internal battles.

Perhaps they love you but do not know how to show you because they are feeling unlovable and unloved. Love and accept them.

Accept yourself and your imperfections. There is more to you than your sickness, your current mental state, your relationship status, your money, your social status or your wealth. There's more to you than what is visible to other people.

Appreciate and enjoy amazing experiences when they happen. What you are grateful for will elicit warm feelings toward yourself. Be grateful for your ability to inhale and exhale. There's beauty even in the simplest acts that show you are living creature. They include breathing in and out and sensing your existence.

Sometimes looking for good is hard work. Imagine what other people lack but you have, and there begins your gratitude. Accept yourself, and your life, as you exist. It is not time to take the exit.

Chapter 6: Values as Antidotes to Quitting

What's your priority in life? Is it wealth, good health, family, education, or travelling? To ascertain your priority, it is important to clarify your values.

Decide which values shape your life and abide by them. Your values will determine which step you take to end "the do-life-or-quit-life dilemma." They determine your level of reverence for life. When your actions conflict with your deeply held values, you go into war with yourself and it is hard to attain inner peace. This phenomenon is known as cognitive dissonance.

Since your values define who you are, take a moment to reflect on them. Consider these questions:

- How are values associated with the problems in my life?
- How do values influence my decision to keep living?

Check out the list of 10 values below. Note if some of them are in your above-mentioned list.

See how they can apply to you and gauge whether they can help you make decisions about your life.

1. **Peacefulness**

Related values: harmony, serenity, tranquillity, calmness.

Whether things are not unfolding the way you want them to, as you do not have power over the universe, be peaceful. When you find peace, you will love to live despite hardships. A lack of peace leads to subconscious attempts to ruin the peace of the people around you. You take it out on others. Peaceful people do not like such kind of company. It is no surprise that without inner peace you might decide to quit life.

Minimize the pursuit of vain things like pointless clashes with others. Minimize interactions with loud and aggressive people. They will interfere with your peace. Seek calm and silence often. Maintain good terms with people and be a good listener. Speak your truth respectfully even if they will not understand you. Remember these people also have their own story.

You don't want to die; you want relief, you want peace, and you want the struggle to end. Grip relief and peace. Peace comes where it is welcomed. Be at peace with the fact that you are here. Be gentle with yourself, forge your own pace, and find peace in silence. Be at peace with being misunderstood. Be at peace with your scars. Be at peace with who you are. Be at peace with yourself and others. *(Create a list of issues that you need to be at peace with.)*

2.   Contentment
Related values: satisfaction, fulfilment, happiness.

The world pushes you to pursue more material wealth and fame than you need. These momentary pleasures are often accompanied by fake love or friendship, many real enemies, and leave no time for fulfilling personal relationships. There's nothing wrong with being famous and pursuing money and riches. However, you can have all you want in the world and still be unhappy, lonely or unable to handle all the stress that comes with it.

One of the keys to happiness is being contented with what you have now. Do what you can with what you have. Comparing the state of your inner life with the outer life of other people is a waste of time.

Focus on what makes your own life great. If possible use your time in service to others who are also having a hard time with the journey. Sharing breeds fulfilment and contentment, unlike selfishness.

3. Determination
Related values: grit, willpower, ambition, aspiration, steadfastness.

Pursuing what you enjoy to do and doing it with enthusiasm improves the fun experience of life. Be determined to make it through. Keep moving despite feeling like you have to surrender. Live this life to the end.

You can give your life and the people in your life the best, but there's no guarantee it shall be returned. It can work in a completely negative way, but give it your best. According to your power and circumstances, life is worth living and you can live it despite harsh circumstances.

Give it your best. Your life is your mark in the world. Be determined to face it bravely while alive. You can only gain experience in determination when you are alive. When going through a horrible situation don't allow it to prevent you from pursuing success. You can die without doing anything, or you can choose to die while still fighting to live. Be determined to overcome obstacles.

4. Perseverance

Related values: fortitude, endurance, tolerance, patience, determination.

Your future might look hopeless and your life like a pending storm ready to burst from the clouds. Nonetheless, you are made with the capability to tolerate, persevere and endure. Many people have tapped into this ability and used it to overcome the most seemingly hopeless of situations. You can too.

For now, you have forgotten that you can harness this ability. Life needs some exercises to keep you in shape and help you fight on. Sometimes it might be clear that there's no way out other than a deadly outcome.

You can always take another option apart from ending your life.

Do not restrict your thoughts of the future. Do not condemn yourself to the fixed attitude that small thoughts bring such as believing you can't do it or there is no hope. As long as you are still here breathing, there's hope. When you cease breathing, the hope dies.

5. Courage

Related values: bravery, fearlessness, grit, fortitude, valour.

Be courageous and fight for your life until you make it. Even if this means fighting against your desires for death. Have the courage to recognize your limitations especially in terms of what you are capable of changing and what is beyond your control.

There's nothing that can guarantee you a happy and successful life all through. Living takes courage. When problems overwhelm you, hope can disappear.

To get going on this critical path of life you have to be courageous enough to overcome obstacles. There's nothing new about problems, and although you feel alone in them, you are not alone.
Other people have faced similar challenges. Some managed through them. Some failed, and some died trying to manage them.

Courage hails from wisdom. You need the courage to accept what you cannot change and to change what you cannot accept. You are running on misplaced courage—more courage to die than to live; more courage to stay the same instead of changing.

Redirect your courage to living. Some people believe the choice to quit living implies cowardice. Do you? Ending your own life requires courage, but living requires even more courage.

6.   Kindness
Related values: hospitality, sympathy, generosity, helpfulness, consideration.

Be good to all people, despite their social, economic, racial or ethnic background. Social relationships add to the purpose of life. No matter where you are, even in prison, you can influence someone else's life positively.

Love others despite their weaknesses. Be good to others even when people mock you for it and assume you have ulterior motives. Be helpful. Kindness with self and others contributes to your happiness and satisfaction in life. People need help, but they may not take it nicely.
Everyone will not appreciate your kindness, but some will. Help not for commendation, but because every human life is important and It is within your power to do so. Being selfish is not joyous. Giving is joyous.

7.   **Honesty**

Related values: integrity, sincerity, openness, truthfulness, trustworthiness, loyalty.

Psychological and spiritual healing requires you to be honest, open and sincere. You will not get better when you hide your symptoms or refuse to go nude for medical examination or injections during a visit to the doctor.

Firstly, be open with yourself and then with the other person who can help you. You have to be real with yourself. Release the burden that is weighing you down. Be sincere about things you have a hard time accepting or letting go.

Don't say, "I don't care what people think of me" when you know you care. Don't be afraid of honesty because it makes you vulnerable. This will cause discomfort in your mind (cognitive dissonance) because you know the truth.

Healing begins with sincere unmasking and honest identification of your distorted thoughts and self-destructive habits. How have you been deceiving yourself?
Perhaps you have been telling yourself lies like "There's nothing I can do." You can do a lot and be successful. You must choose the right action. Be truthful to yourself.

8. Resilience

Related values: adaptability, flexibility, endurance, strength.

Resilience is both a skill and a value. You can become strong again after stressful times. You are part of nature like the trees, the stars, the animals, and the seas. Observing nature you will find out that all living things strive to remain alive. They adapt, and they become resilient to the hardships they face.

Do you have a reason to be here or not? Just as the plants and animals, you occupy space on this planet. No one else can occupy that space the way you do. Can you not let yourself be changed for the worse under difficult situations? Can you stay focused on your goals despite the challenges? Of course, you can.

9. Persistence

Related values: commitment, consistency, determination.

How do you often react when things go wrong in your life? Instead of giving up, form a habit of persistence. Persist until you achieve something. You may fail, but you may win.

Despite failing to be what it purports to be or what you want it to be, being alive is what it is. Persistence will make you realize that your life is worthy.

Being alive is beautiful in itself when all other factors do not complicate it. You are born with an innate desire to live and that's why we have the natural propensity to fight for our life or to flee from life-threatening situations even when it means to die while fighting.

10. Self-discipline

Related values: self-control, focus, prudence, willpower, temperance.

You cannot attain the life you desire without discipline. Self-discipline keeps you alive. No one can be disciplined for you. You have to practice being self-disciplined until it becomes your way of life.

Have you been in a situation where you plan to do something but then you lose the enthusiasm to do it? What happens then? Do you still do it or do you brush it aside because you no longer feel like doing it? Discipline means being focused and sticking to what you had planned to do even when you don't feel enthusiastic about doing it anymore. Self-discipline will help you to keep living even when you no longer feel enthusiastic about living anymore.

Chapter 7: Belonging to Humanity

Some say your life belongs to the universe, not to you personally. What do you say? The universe as we know it is a vast thing, always expanding, and its limit is infinity. It is massive and never-ending giving the impression of having secrets which one human being cannot discover within the normal lifespan.

Considering the enormity of the universe, one human being is a mere speck seeming insignificant. Nonetheless, humanity is also infinite and one human being cannot discover all the secrets of humanity unless they live forever.

As drops of water form an ocean, individual humans form humanity. We exist in this universe alongside other phenomena. You belong to humanity.

Your desire to belong is a normal human desire. Psychologists (e.g. Abraham Maslow) have identified belonging as an important need for our survival.

Having people you care about and who care about you improves the quality of your life. It is clear how big the value of family and friendship in life is.

As a result, when you feel like you lack social ties in your life, life feels unworthy. Or when you think you don't get approval from your social circle or society, you may lose your love for life. All human beings don't want the best for us. Not all human beings are meant for us but, humanity, in general, is precious and you are part of it.

Responsibility to Others

How is your relationship with your family and friends? Are you always lonely? Do you feel like a foreigner in your own home? It is horrible to feel out of place and not accepted by people.

It is heart-breaking when your closeness or sense of attachment with the people you consider important in your life, is broken. You feel like you have lost your identity or have been rejected.

Loneliness is the immense feeling that arises when you lack identity because of a poor sense of belonging. You feel like a perpetual misfit.

Perhaps you are misunderstood, unaccepted, underestimated, rejected or humiliated. You find it impossible to form any union with anything, anyone or any group of people. Lacking belongingness like this leads to hopelessness.

What happens when the bonds you have forged break because of human imperfections or death?

Does it mean that your worth, respect, and confidence are gone forever?

When relationships fail and affiliations stop, when you are abandoned and feel out of place, don't be frustrated to a point of no return.

Authentically and honestly evaluate your expectations of others and your expectations of yourself.

You need people, but you also need to be with yourself, by yourself and for yourself. You desire for belonging does not negate your need for individuality.

At times it is important to enjoy solitude and be happy with your own company. You can be alone but not lonely. Spend alone time not to pity, but to develop yourself.

Stars are wonderfully made. Stars die, but they keep shining to the end. After their death, they might leave behind a black hole. The black hole proclaims of its former powerful presence. You are like a star.

You are wonderfully made. Keep shining to the end. Do life as much as you can for as long as you can. Death will come, and you will leave behind a black hole. You don't need to hasten it by suicide.

Be at Peace with Being Misunderstood

When a few people around you misunderstand you, it feels like no one in the world understands you or your situation. The more you tell yourself this lie the more you will believe it.

It is currently estimated that more than 7 billion people live on earth. What do you mean when you say "nobody understands?" Out of all these people, some have been in the same situation as you are. Some people will soon experience similar challenges.

When you conclude that nobody understands, is the statement authentic?

"No one understands" is a phrase distorted by our propensity to look at things from only one perspective. You have not met everybody. Be more specific.

Who exactly does not understand? Why do you think this person does not understand? Have they been through what you are going through right now?

Understand it is difficult for people to know exactly what you are feeling inside if they have not been through it. Give people the benefit of doubt.
You don't understand everyone either especially if you have never experienced the kind of struggles they have. Unless you have experienced it, it is tough to understand it.

Do you understand why some people do not understand you? If your answer is 'no' to this question then why expect them to understand? People will always misunderstand. People have a different point of view, and everybody does not think as you do.

Are you feeling misunderstood? Expect nothing less than that. Everyone will not sympathize with your plight. Everyone will not understand what you are going through. It doesn't necessarily mean they are unkind or blind to your suffering. Therefore, appreciate their well-meaning attempts to assist you even though you may think they are not helpful or comforting enough.

Expecting people to understand you through and through is irrational when you do not open up entirely to the person you expect to understand. If you want to be understood, be more understanding. You will enjoy more relaxed relationships. Therefore, live peacefully with others, leave other people's lives alone and mind yours.

Find a purpose from the experience of being misunderstood. For instance, be the one who understands people who are misunderstood.
Looking for inspiration in your negative experiences is a positive way to look at life. The issue you feel strongly about could be your source of inspiration to do life.

Sometimes you have to speak out, reach out to these people so that they can know you are going through hectic times. Don't just expect them to see. Don't assume it is obvious to them just because it is obvious to you. People see what they want to see based on their own situation. Understand yourself first. Some people understand the psychological pain you might be going through. Some people have thought about ending their lives too.

The World Health Organisation (WHO) estimated that over 800,000 people (as of 2018) worldwide commit suicide every year. The number is larger when you consider those who thought about it but did not go through with it.

Someone somewhere understands. The problem is in finding this person who understands.

Therefore, my recommendation to you would be to make this person yourself before you look for understanding externally.

Other people might not know exactly what you are feeling. What you understand about what you are feeling is the most important thing for you. Try speaking up.
Choose your audience wisely. Let it be someone you respect. Talk to a significant other or a professional counsellor.

You cannot keep silent and expect people to understand the pain that you are going through. Everyone is busy with their struggles. Hence, lower your expectations. Seek instead to understand others first.

How to Restore a Sense of Belongingness
Note which statements describe your life:
- No one cares about me.
- I will never amount to anything.
- The world/people will be better off without me.
- It doesn't matter whether I live or die.
- I lack involved people e.g. parents, guardians, spouse, family, friends et cetera.
- I lack a positive identity of myself.
- I can't do anything right.
- I am overwhelmed with all this pressure.
- I can't handle this kind of life.

Note which of these give you a sense of belonging:
- Feeling/being wanted
- Feeling/being appreciated
- Feeling/being loved
- Feeling/being accepted
- Feeling/being recognized

- Feeling/being needed
- Feeling/being admired

Other people can only give you the above to a limited degree. Give yourself what you wish to be given by others. This list can jog your mind.

- Self-acceptance
- Self-admiration
- Self-appreciation
- Self-confidence
- Self-esteem
- Self-knowledge
- Self-love
- Self-trust
- Self-worth
- Self-reliance
- Self-respect
- Self-recognition

Unlearn your dependence on others to make you feel like you belong. Learn how to belong to yourself first. Treat yourself the way you want to be treated before you expect others to make you feel like you belong. Don't sit waiting for people to serve you happiness. Does it work like that? No, life demands that you work toward achieving your happiness because it is an inner state.

Always say this to yourself whenever you feel less human and your sense of belonging is diminished:

"I am a human being and nothing can take this away from me."

"I am a human being and no one can take this away from me."

"I am a human being and I will not take this away from me."

Your race, ethnicity, deformity, or illness doesn't define you. You are not your illness, your race, your height, weight, or social status. You are not just a body. You are more than that.

Never give up searching for what you can do despite the frustrations you experience in life. Though your current condition might be frustrating, you can do something with yourself.

If you can't see it, then make it a goal to keep living until you find it. Not seeing the meaning of life now, is not equivalent to its non-existence. It means you are not seeing it at the moment, but given some time, you will.

You belong to humanity. Humanity is bigger than socially acclaimed statuses and societal definitions of the ideal person. The entire humankind is here because of life. Therefore, you belong to life. Avoid looking at other people as "they."

- "They don't understand me."
- "They expect me to be perfect."
- "They don't want me."

It nurtures a sense of isolation. Use "we." Accept your oneness with humanity.

- We can understand.
- We are not perfect.
- We are important.

Here is one tip to help you make worthwhile decisions. Ask yourself, "if everyone decides to do what I am about to do, where will humanity be?"

Never underrate the negative influence that a hampered sense of affection or affiliation can cause on your psychological state.

Train your mind to fulfil this need by acknowledging your affiliation to enormous and long-lasting phenomena like humanity, our earth, our solar system or the galaxy.

Take time to learn about the world. You do not need to be a scientist to enjoy looking at the amazing heavenly bodies and the wonders of the universe.

Observing on a wider angle helps to put things into perspective. Case in point, take time to observe nature. Start watching National Geographic videos and see how mere animals struggle for survival because life is meant to be lived.

No matter what happens to you, you can survive through your effort rather than die through your effort. Try this: next time someone offends you or diminishes your worth, go out and lie down facing the sky's expanse. You might realize how small the problem is. As long as you are not harming another precious human life, you have no reason to fear society's perception of you.

It is amazing and awe-inspiring to view the majestic elements of nature such as the human body, planets, moons, sky, stars, seas, animals, landscapes among others. No matter how alone and isolated you feel, you are a part of nature. You are a human being. As long as you exist, there's nothing anyone can do to deny you your humanness—unless you are brainwashed into thinking otherwise.

Your humanness is a fixed phenomenon. A human being with any other name is still a being on earth possessing human capabilities. (Call yourself Earthian if you want.) The components of your body are similar to the components of Earth. Your own body belongs to Earth. You are an earthen being. You belong to life since you are a living being in a vast universe, an enormous planet. You are part of a Higher Order.

Everything else is futile.

Your appearance might be different from the ordinary expectation of the normal human being. You are born different and you experience life differently from others, but you are still a human being. You are matter. Matter occupies space. The specific place you occupy in the world is yours alone. You matter.

You do not have to join a gang or a cult to feel like you belong. You can join other groups or organizations which lobby for the improvement of humanity. However, relying on groups to define who you are can lead to more problems. It is limiting to choose a small group you want to belong to and allow it to define everything about you. You are so much more than your social affiliations. You are a member of living organisms.

People need you sometimes. The moment you are born, you have a role in society. You might lose sight of this during a crisis. If you are a parent or son/daughter, people need you. In the unfortunate situation where you have lost everyone, then you are the chance to rescue a generation. Every living thing is capable of reproducing. By quitting, you willingly kill an entire generation.

With life, there's always hope and there is always a way. While some orphans lack parents, some parents lack children. Even when your productiveness has been thwarted, you can take care of another who lacks.

Human beings can progress together to great heights by taking care of each other's lack. Make your life worth living by impacting on those around you in whatever way you can. Humanity is about offering kind service to other humans. There's joy in sharing what you can with others even if what you have to offer is little.

Just get out there and smile at a stranger. A slight lingering smile which will charm instead of scare. Remind other people they are important because they belong to life. Take the first step to show others they belong even if they belong to a group of misfits.

A lack of a sense of belonging is distressing, but it is not worth losing your life for. Find a reason to stay alive in your lack of belonging. Which is to discover the importance of living.

Death will come someday, but may it not be by your own hand. Find something you enjoy doing and focus until you achieve it. Don't kill yourself before you try. Try evading death and fighting suicidal thoughts, and other life-threatening situations. (I encourage you to seek the help of a trained mental health professional when you become tired of fighting death and life is overwhelming.) We live to fight death. That's the reason why institutions like religions, hospitals, and prisons try to save lives. We belong together because we have a mutual thing to do, namely life.

Chapter 8: The Burden of Being a Burden

Do you believe you are a burden to people? Do you regard yourself as a weight to those who are helping you?

It is tiring to your mind when you fill it with vexations and the ideas that you are a burden to others. It is worse when you consider yourself to be a burden to yourself.

The thought of being a burden is a burden to the mind. It is often accompanied by worthlessness and helplessness. It is tough when you believe you are a burden. Your perception is you are a cause of pain and suffering, a burden to people.

You want to live, but you feel like you do not deserve to. In such a state it is hard to appreciate your life's worth. Life loses its sanctity in your eyes, and you become less committed to it. You can easily reason that people will be better off without you.

There are other ways of lowering your possibility of being a burden apart from killing yourself. First, analyse your situation keenly—are you a burden, or are you perceiving yourself as a burden?

Consider the burden that you will leave behind to the people who will have to deal with the aftermath of your suicide. The people who will find your body in a position that appears to be an apparent suicide and they have to carry it.

It will be a real burden to them, not self-perceived. People will experience situational distress knowing you ended your life intentionally. The emotional burden you leave behind might be bigger than the burden you perceive yourself to be at the moment.

If you have a family or friends, they will be tormented by guilt. Death by suicide leaves behind confusion to your loved ones and other affected people as well. You can prevent leaving a physical and mental burden to them by staying alive and doing whatever you can to stay alive.

Even though you perceive yourself as a burden, which is not a wrong perception sometimes, it is good to ask for help and accept it when offered. The ego likes acting like it does not need anyone, and yet you do need people.

You are not on this earth alone and we are here to assist each other. The current situation of another person could be your future situation. For example, we grow old and become physically or mentally ill. Make peace with the fact that you need fellow human beings. In death and life, we need other people.

Unfortunately, some people will tell you straight to your face that you are a burden to them. Such sharp words can cut like a sword, but don't take them to heart. People usually feel so sometimes, and it is heart-breaking if these people are your family members.

Here is the thing, you are still alive because you can live. Your presence matters. No one else can be present for you. Live for you. No one can live for you. Often, your circumstances, like illness or disability, can cause you to consider yourself a burden. Do life even if it means the action of living is all that you can do.

When you were born, guess who showed up? Keep showing up for life to occupy the space you have been given above the ground. Fight to keep living.

Accept help and be grateful for it when you get it. If you are blessed with people who are willing to help, let them.

Most people find comfort in helping others. When you are blessed with such a person, be grateful. When friends or family members are willing to support you, accept their help.
Sometimes they might be total strangers. If it is within your ability, pay for help. Pay for services from domestic cleaners, caregivers, personal nurses, counsellors and so forth.

You will be supporting them, and they will be supporting you. Also, contact an organization dealing with your issue or form one if it is non-existent.

Let them help you and gift them with your presence on earth. Perhaps helping you gives them a reason to live, and they believe it is their purpose.

Be grateful for those who are willing to offer assistance in whatever way they can. Talk to your loved ones and thank them for all they do for you.
In a world where everyone is already special, it is easy to go unnoticed and feel invisible. On a wider perspective: the core thing making you perceive your life as a burden to others, is the reason for you to feel special.

Chapter 9: Regaining Capability for Life

Quitting life begins with thoughts. You start to think about suicide and regularly entertain suicidal thoughts before making the decision. After sustaining the thought of quitting life, you reason that death by suicide is the only option you have.

Gradually, you might begin to engage in reckless and self-harming behaviours like cutting yourself, starving, addictions, promiscuous sex, or putting yourself in danger intentionally. You might not have the courage to quit life on your own. Thereby you keep putting yourself in harm's way hoping that someone can kill you. Or you knowingly engage in risky behaviours. At this point, you can still change and go back to a state of loving life with proper help and support.

At birth, every helpless new-born has a capability for life. Life is a feast, and they have a great appetite. Not knowing the ills of the world, the child takes life as it is. As children grow older, they begin to realize that life is not always good. Sometimes upsetting experiences are hard for their developed mind to forget. Their inborn survival instincts decrease and the likelihood of losing their appetite for life increases.

Some manage to develop resilience to the hard life, but others lose their appetite for life completely. Our inborn capability for life is shrouded by the challenges we undergo. We get the justification to quit life. Suicide looks like the most reasonable option we can imagine. We acquire a capability for suicide. Our initial capability for life reduces. The original will to live is replaced with the will to die.

Many people think about committing suicide, but not all of them end up killing themselves. What differs? They regain their capability for life by willing themselves to live despite the challenges they encounter.

Recurrent exposure to dangerous situations, traumatic experiences or access to lethal means gradually gives you the capability to end your own life.

Engaging in self-harming and reckless behaviours ruins your natural capability to sustain your own life. Your alienation from life increases. You become a threat to yourself.

Hence, you might be afraid of yourself because you have the potential to end your own life. It is like you have replaced your survival instincts with suicidal instincts. Living things naturally strive to live, but now you are striving to die.

Safety Planning

All hope is not lost. It is hard, but not impossible to do life when your capability to live has reduced. You must take steps to lower your capability to quit life and increase your capability to do life. If it is difficult to do it on your own, you can approach a counsellor or a spiritual mentor.

To protect your life from yourself, create a safety plan that can help you deal. Make an agreement with yourself and accomplish it. A safety plan will minimize the risk of harming yourself.

Memorize it, write it on a card or notebook that you can keep in your pocket or save in your phone. Keep it with you at all times. You might need help with this. Do not fear seeking help from willing people.

Include the following elements in your safety plan:
1. Contact details of family members, friends, counsellors, or significant others you can talk to
2. Your local suicide hotline number
3. The nearest hospital you can go to during a crisis
4. Contact details of your mental health provider
5. Reminders to reduce your access to lethal items

6. Reminders, mementoes, pictures of significant people or good moments in your life
7. A list of reasons for living
8. Encouraging quotations like philosophical quotes, Bible verses, or self-assuring phrases

Sometimes the only plan you need is to continue living and see what happens. *Qui sera, sera.* Whatever will be, will be. Safety planning is useful for easing *Psychache* and reminding your mind of your inborn capability for life.

Chapter 10: Alternatives to Quitting Life

Death by suicide might seem very appealing due to the idea that it will bring instant relief. However, life is not the only thing you must quit. Look keenly in all directions before resorting to a decision that will wipe you out of the face of the earth.

What is the point of destroying yourself when your battery is not dead yet? Your heart has not given up beating, why force it to stop?

Despite what you are going through at this moment, as long as you are alive, you can regain your joy for living. Killing yourself cuts out all your chances of having a bright future. There's always another way.

You are walking on the road, and you see someone trying to kill himself.

- You are in a position to help.
- Would you help?
- If you see someone in danger of losing their life, you will do your best to try to change their mind (unless you are a psychopath.)
- Deep down you know human life deserves to be saved.

Do life because you are worthy enough to be alive. You can still be alive. At times when under a lot of stress it is difficult to see beyond your problems. The *Psychache* directs your focus to one direction, yet there are so many alternative paths your life can take. Quitting is not the only way. There's always another alternative to quitting life. Continue living to find it.

Seeking Help

Do something about your troubles which does not involve ending your own life. Imagine you are talking to yourself as another person. Now, give yourself good advice that supports life.

Help yourself to become the person that you can be. You can keep living through the help of other people. Help from others can only work when you are willing to receive it.

Keep seeking help and you shall find it. Where can you find help? Through psychological guidance which is offered by counsellors; in organizations that promote causes that are relevant to your situation; through supportive family, friends or strangers.
Read readily available inspirational stories from around the world. Listen to other people when they share their challenges and methods they used to overcome.
Find out how other people are beating the odds to keep living. The experiences of fellow human beings can help you to gain another perspective toward life.

What to Quit instead of Quitting Life

Quit habits that threaten your peace of mind.

If your desire to end your life is so strong that it seems achievable, what about the smaller things? Shouldn't they be easier to quit? Quit aspects of life that are smaller than life. You don't need to quit life, but you need to quit toxic habits, situations and people who threaten your peace of mind. Life is bigger than aggressive people, avoidable drama, gossip, slander, anger and other trivialities. It is not time to end your life. It is time to end things that are ruining our life. Quit self-destructive habits. Quit dwelling on negative suicidal thoughts.

Have you already established a habit of giving up? Are you in the process of establishing a habit of giving up? What habits in your life do you feel ashamed of?

You must quit those, not your life. Quit the habit of quitting when things get tough or complex.
Find the balance between knowing when to keep holding on and knowing when to let go, knowing what to do and knowing what to quit.

Begin every new chapter of your life by eliminating factors which increase your risk of quitting life. Choose constructive habits, situations and people.

Quit expecting people to behave the way they're supposed to.

Why do you expect people to act in a certain way for your sake? You expect them to behave in a way you think they are supposed to. You expect them to know what to say, when and where to say it. You expect too much from others who do not know exactly what you are feeling at the moment.

They might not always say or do the right thing at the right time. Maybe they also are expecting the same from you. Treat people the way you wish them to treat you and leave it at that. Do for others what you expect them to do for you. Be what you expect others to be.

There is great freedom in letting people be when they are not listening to your point of view rather than trying to force them to get you.

Quit telling yourself how people are "supposed to" behave toward you. People will disappoint you.
God has given every human being the freedom to choose how to live their life, to think for themselves and to make their own decisions.

You were not put on earth to live up to everyone's expectations. Do what you are supposed to according to the role life has given you and hope the other person will do their part.

Consequently, quit expecting people to be enslaved to your expectations of them. Care most about who you are to yourself and how you behave toward yourself, instead of focusing too much on who you are to others. People cannot stop your pain and grief for you.

Quit expecting people to always please you. Quit expecting people to get rid of your grief. Quit expecting to be treated the way you always want to be treated. Quit expecting perfection from people who are just human beings like you. Quit expecting everyone to behave in a way that benefits you. Quit expecting everyone to understand. Instead, seek to understand yourself first, then behave in a way that will benefit your life.

Quit being controlled by the ego.

Pride encompasses perfectionism, arrogance, and selfishness—the so-called ego. If you have to kill something then kill pride. The type of pride found in the proverb that states "pride comes before a fall."
It is the elevation of the self until others are seen as less important. Pride is a deceptive power that blocks you from admitting your mistakes and compels you to refuse help when you need it.

Pride will make it hard for you to listen to well-meaning advice and other viewpoints. It gives you a sense of exaggerated self-importance and causes you to have negative attitudes toward yourself and other people. With time pride is a source of sorrow and loneliness.

Quit comparing yourself to others out of competition and the desire to appear like you are above other human beings.

Be delighted of yourself and your accomplishments, but let them not get into your head so much that you despise others who have not reached there yet. Pride has driven awesome people who seem to have a successful life to commit suicide when they have to climb down the ladder. They feared being seen as less than perfect.

You can always rise from failure, as long as you do not commit suicide. Replace your pride with humility, compassion and empathy.

Quit denying God's presence.

You have a spiritual need. That's why we are different from animals. In all cultures, from time immemorial, human beings have been seeking to fulfil their spiritual needs. Pursue your spiritual well-being by seeking a good relationship with God. Scientists have so far confirmed life has to spring up from existing life. God is the source of life.

We use stuff that different kinds of engineers have created. We likely don't know these engineers; never see them, hear them, cross paths with them. Nevertheless, we know they exist, because of what they have created and how useful their innovations are to us. They put in the work to make things easier for us. In the same way, we are God's innovation. You are alive today because of God's will.

Maybe you identify with an old bridge which is so torn that you feel like the engineer that made you has forgotten you. You feel like you are going to disintegrate anytime and think you can't live anymore. You do not have to wait for help, you can ask for help.

With time you will die. Nonetheless, now that you are here and you are still functional don't lose your faith in your Creator. Seek help from Him. Take time to observe His awesome creations including yourself. Quit denying the powerful presence of the engineer who made you.

Quit living in the past.

What emotional hurt have you been carrying from the past? Is it helpful to live in a "what-you-could-have-done" state?

Do what you can now. When you realize something that you regret doing or saying, take relevant action.

Forgive or ask for forgiveness. Living in the present moment with a mindset fixed on the past cannot result in a peaceful state of mind. Let the bad past experiences be lessons you can apply today rather than regrets for a lifetime. Your past does not define you, but you can use it to refine you.

Address all your hurts because holding on to them will lead to bad choices. It is hard to make rational choices when you are holding on to pain. It is hard to see a reason for living when you are constantly replaying your miseries through daily conversations, or in your thoughts.

Quit holding on to hurt. Quit spending all your attention in an old place you can never go back to.

Quit trying to impress everyone.

Your life is more important than societal stigma and people's opinion of you. Some of the people who you are trying to impress will be happy when they see you fail.

Live life in a way that you harm no one and be mindful of the people who care about you. Do not live to impress everyone at the expense of your inner peace. Live to impress God. Life will become more stressful when you live for the sake of what impression you give people. Be okay with who you are. People will judge you even when they don't know you.

Be at peace with being criticised as long as you know what you are doing is right. Do you live by standards that other people set for you about how you are supposed to act, think, and behave? If yes, then you are their slave.

Do you take all the advice that comes your way or do you carefully think and ignore some? You are free to do as you please, but remember that you must be ready to face the consequences of your actions. It is irrational to try to please everybody, even if you love them. Quit giving people the power to control your inner self. Regain control and power over yourself. Quit waiting for approval, give yourself approval.

Quit trying to control what you cannot control.

Life becomes tougher than necessary when you try to control the uncontrollable. Take steps to change what you can change and accept what you cannot change. Some things are beyond your control, but oftentimes you try to control these things.

Trying to control what other people think of you is like trying to control gravity. You do not have control over many things that happen to you or around you. To prevent undue disappointments, identify what you cannot control and let it be. The only person you can control is yourself.

Often, you think things are beyond your control when they are within your reach. It takes wisdom, knowledge of life, and courage to accept your limits.

You might experience painful circumstances due to natural disasters or accidents that you have no control over. Other people's choices cause pain. For example, when a crime is committed against you, or when people betray your trust.

You ought to be aware of your ability to change and control things. In the end, you are responsible for what you can control. If there is a chance of doing something about it, do it. For instance, seeking legal action, making changes, or forgiving and accepting life as it is.

Quit the victim mentality.

Quit being a prisoner of a fixed negative mindset. Quit rumination and talking negativity into your life. Otherwise, it will ruin your life, relationships, and mental peace. A victim mentality is characterized by Sympathy-seeking behaviour, self-pity, and pessimism.

Also, blaming other people for the consequences of your own choices and the inability to take responsibility for your actions. It is an obsession with talking about your limitations and other people's weaknesses.

The victim mentality makes you poor at showing empathy to others. For instance, when someone starts to talk to you about their problem, you start telling them about your problem too. A victim mentality is established when you constantly complain and tell everyone about your pitiful story without doing anything to change the situation.

Do you choose to be an owner of life or a victim of life? Do you choose to be victorious or defeated? Spend time with people who value peace and positive thinking.

Even though you may have gone through an ordeal in which you were a victim, be kind to yourself by not letting it define who you are. It is therapeutic to talk about your problems, but useless to make them a topic for all conversations.

Quit being a difficult person to deal with.

Be open to correction. Be open to new experiences when things change. You are a difficult person to deal with when nothing pleases you even when your family or friends try.

Or you find fault in everything they do or say to you even though you know they had well-meaning intentions. You act out easily out of intensified emotions, and it is hard to calm you down. Or you try to manipulate and control people to do what you want without listening to their opinion.

For example, you may hate the phrase "life goes on" when you are facing grief. It might not be comforting enough because the intense pain makes it seem like you cannot go on. Avoid being so quick to get angry when people give you such clichéd phrases.

It is good to appreciate when people are simply trying to be nice to you even if according to your standards they are failing. Quit being hard to deal with.

Quit fearing to seek assistance.

It is difficult to achieve much without the help of family, friends, colleagues, classmates, counsellors and even strangers. Listen to all advice, but pick the advice that will be in the best interests of your life. If anyone shows interest in helping you and you need it, seize that opportunity. When you open up to someone and they do not seem to get it, refuse to get worked up over it.

Sometimes your loved ones will not identify with your lack of enthusiasm for life. Some will not understand your mental anguish.

What you consider an anthill, another will consider a mountain and the inverse is true. However, you can always find someone who will listen with objectivity and care.
You have the option of looking for counsellors or psychotherapists if you cannot find an understanding friend or family member to talk to.

They can connect you with a support group comprising of people with problems like yours. Remember to return the favour. Listen and help people who you have reason to believe are suffering.

Also, do not forsake the value of prayer. Who knows you best than your Creator? Some people in your circle cannot be trusted with your concerns. They can make things worse. You can trust The Most High with your intimate concerns and burdens.

Chapter 11: Make the Decision to Do Life

Circumstances might encumber you during your journey through this critical path of life. Once you know how to handle yourself during tough storms, you will be able to handle life as it is. However, if you choose to quit living you will never know. The wisdom of life involves knowing how to make decisions. Apply the following tips when making decisions in your life.

Decide to preserve life.

What's your history with quitting life? Attempting suicide in the past puts you at greater risk of attempting again. How many times have you attempted to quit and what saved your life? Engaging in physically injurious behaviour and self-inflicted harm can develop the desire to end it all, or result in accidental suicide.

Therefore, depending on your personal needs, take proper measures to keep yourself safe. (Refer to Chapter 9 under Safety Planning.) The decision to do life rather than quit needs bravery and courage. It requires believing deeply that you have a responsibility to yourself and others (like your parents, spouse, children, and humanity.)

The only way to fulfil this responsibility is by choosing life. Protect and preserve all life, including your own.

Decide to manage thoughts of quitting.

Having the thought to end your life does not mean you will do it. The frequency of the thoughts matters. The more you dwell on suicidal thoughts, the more they will advance and impede your ability to think about another way out.

Wishing for death can make you decide to intentionally put yourself in dangerous situations so that you can be killed. You can only find a reason to live if you find a way to manage these thoughts. It takes a lot of effort and proper intervention strategies to battle suicidal thoughts.

Decide to manage stress.

Recent stressful situations in your life may invoke intense, unendurable emotions to the extent that you wish to quit life. What stressors have you encountered recently?

Stress is an exercise for the mind like physical exercise to the body. It makes you uncomfortable and helps you to develop mental strength. Stressful times can be growth opportunities, but you have to choose to look at them as such.

In life, you will be cheated, ignored, betrayed, and disappointed. Your hopes will be shattered and your dreams will fail to materialize.

Decide to manage your stressors and cope with the problems of life effectively. Life is meant to be lived. Decide to grow through what you are going through. Stress is unavoidable. Be open to learning from your stressors.

Decide to sustain worthy relationships with others.

Feeling connected to other people can reduce your stress. When you lack social connectedness, this might point you in the direction of giving up. Sometimes people think they are alone or that others will be better off without them. Do you ever feel this way? We always need others, sometimes we need to swallow our pride and accept help, especially if this help gives us the chance to continue living.

Decide to seek professional counselling.

Some uninformed people often spit out depression and suicide like it is nothing. However, it is advisable not to assume that depression is the only cause of suicide. If you can afford psychotherapy, look for the services of mental health professionals.

Avoid self-diagnosing yourself with any mental illness until it has been confirmed by a professional. Keep in mind that psychotherapy is a process and it is not mere advice-giving.

You can find advice everywhere. Many books out there claiming to have the answers to all your life problems. If you take or trust every advice which you find online or you are given by friends, you will become crooked.

Everyone has something to teach you. Hence, think of the consequences before you follow pieces of advice. The only person who will live with the ultimate consequence of your actions is yourself.

Why reach out to people who have appropriate clinical training to handle mental health crises?

The individual without training will easily bring in personal biases and might be dealing with mental issues which they have not dealt with.

In an ideal situation, professional mental health workers usually undergo supervision, consultation, debriefing, and other activities which put them in a better position to attend to people with mental health problems. Those are not processes that an ordinary person undergoes.

Therefore, professional therapy is ideally objective and not subject to bias and too much guesswork. Professional mental health care involves less of advice-giving and more conditioning, unlearning and building mental health skills. It also involves follow-ups and the social support of loved ones (who might give advice.)
Check out this brief guide for seeking professional mental health care.

Mental health care professionals
- Psychiatrists
- Psychiatric nurses
- Clinical psychologists
- Psychotherapists
- Counsellors
- Social workers

Where to find them
- Mental health facilities/hospitals
- Hospitals
- Counselling Centres
- Drug rehab centres
- Mental health organizations
- Public mental health institutions
- Online counselling centres

Chapter 12: Express Gratitude

Always find something to be grateful for, no matter how small it may seem. If you can read books or listen to audio, then you have a lot to be grateful for in life.

Frequent gratitude has lasting stress-relieving effects on your mind. Stop taking your life for granted. Despite what you are experiencing now, these are a lot of things you can be grateful for.

Make a list of things, people, and situations you are grateful for. Form a daily habit of identifying things such things. Be specific about it and always keep the list in mind when bombarded with an overwhelming desire to quit life.

Check out the following list of general things you can be grateful for.

1. Be grateful you are a human being despite your imperfections.
Your illness, your flaws, your ethnicity, and your background do not make you less human. You are as human as any other human being. Appreciate that you are capable of doing amazing things and live your time. At this moment, you occupy a space on this planet no one else occupies. It is a tiny place, but a significant place. You are not important to everybody, but your worth is intact. How you reached

here is not important. The fact that you are here is. What makes you wish you were not born? Being alive is a privilege that many have been denied. Some are born dead, some die during birth, but you are still here, being, doing, living, and existing. Do life.

2. Be grateful for your life. You can breathe and your heart is beating. This moment that you are alive is precious because so many have died fighting for their lives. They loved to live, but they died. Let this be your motivation to live because it is a privilege denied to many but you have it. Be grateful for your human life. There are so many other routes your life can take. Being alive at this moment is a blessing to be treasured. As much as life is full of miseries, life itself is bigger than you and yet you are part of it. You are significant despite being a dot in the universe. Appreciate your existence. Do life.

3. Be grateful for your family, friends, or acquaintances. Appreciate people who check on you and are willing to talk to you. Even if they don't check on you as frequently as you expect, you too can check on them. One thing most human beings agree upon is that human life is precious. Normal humans do not like it when they see a stranger dying because it is a reminder of their mortality. Sometimes it seems like no one needs us, yet we play a role in giving others a reason to live. In a way, when you struggle to keep living, you save not only your life but that of others too. Your family, your friends and significant others will not always be here. The best gift you can bestow them with is your presence. Do life.

4. Be grateful when you can meet your physical needs of food, shelter and clothing. Be more grateful if you can fund your hobbies, travel around the world or pay for mental health services. If you lack all these, then may that your reason to live. Keep living so that you can fulfil your needs and those of significant people. When you have everything you need and more, share what you have with others who lack. Life can feel empty when we do not look beyond our needs and mind other people's needs as well. Be grateful for what you have. Do life.

5. Be grateful when you experience inner peace. Your inner peace does not depend on material wealth and external forces, it comes from within. To earn this you have to work hard at it and meet your spiritual needs. No matter how much you strive for richness, fame or other outwardly show of success, you will not be happy unless you achieve spiritual and mental well-being. Material things are important, but they can neither fulfil your spiritual needs nor get rid of psychological pain. When it seems like it is impossible to achieve peace of mind, seek guidance. Find peace. Do life.

Additional purport.

Many people enjoy living despite their terrible conditions. One of the bitter truths of life is that people are managing with worse situations than yours. You may have the ideal life in someone else's eyes, but you lack the joy of living. It is hard for such people to understand why you would want to kill yourself, yet you are living their dream. (Do you see, the necessity to be at peace with being misunderstood?)

The life you are willing to end is being desired by someone elsewhere who has no choice but to succumb to death. Let us borrow a Shakespearean anecdote:

Once a man was pitying himself for not having shoes. Then, he saw another who had no legs. The first man realized that it could have been worse. He did not have a reason to complain anymore. He had what he needed most and someone else was surviving without what he had.

Meditate about this in your own life. What do you have? Starting now, begin appreciating everything you have and stop bemoaning over what you lack. Whatever happens next, you are in control now. Choose wisely.

The pain can end. Your life does not have to. You do not want to die. You want peace, happiness and freedom. Those are states of mind you are capable of achieving. You will figure out alternative ways of achieving them if you don't give up.

Chapter 13: Problem-solving Skills

Do not avoid your problems or your negative feelings. Allow yourself to experience the negativity in your life just as you allow yourself to feel joy when you experience good times. Do not be afraid of the pain, tears, or negative emotions. The purpose of these natural emotions is to communicate about your inner state. Feel them. Stop fighting them. Strive to see what they are communicating to you.

Ignoring the problem neither solves it nor ends it. Face your psychological and emotional pain. That is when the healing journey begins. Face your issues head-on as they come. Use the following guidelines to improve goal-directed coping and problem-solving skills.

Dealing with the Problem

Define the problem.

How you view the problem is the first thing to consider. Because how you deal with it, react to it and decide about it will be derived from how you perceive it.

- What is your major problem right now?
- What have you lost as a result?
- What caused this situation?

- Are you in control of the situation?
- Are you in control of yourself?

Assess the Nature of the problem.
- Identify the causes and triggers
- Identify situations that do not last
- Identify what you cannot change
- Identify the types of losses (such as emotional, financial, physical)
- Mourn your losses

Identify the lessons learnt.
- What have you gained from the experience?
- How can you rise from your current situation?
- What capabilities do you need to rise?
- Do you have these capabilities?
- What can you do to improve on these capabilities?

Find possible solutions.
- Outline possible solutions
- Analyse possible solutions
- Choose the most important thing to do

Take action.

- Take action and put in the effort
- Evaluate if your action is working
- Modify and use other alternatives as needed

Coping with the Problem

Dealing with personal problems involves knowing what to give up despite the cost and knowing what to retain.

Do not be quick to find relief. You will be relieved after you let yourself into the experience without suppressing your painful feelings. Fulfil the need to grieve over your disappointments and losses instead of refusing to mourn.

The problem with choosing suicide as a method of problem-solving is that you are deliberately causing permanent harm to yourself, the person who will handle your body, your family and friends.

Be courageous and strong. Be firm and take a stand in the face of a problem. You can escape some problems before they arrive, but others cannot be dodged. They demand to be faced and dealt with. Do you want to postpone your problems to another date when you will have a collection of other problems?

Recognize this when analysing your situation in the presence of an unbearable problem—when there is no way of avoiding it, or when avoiding it does not solve it, but merely postpones it.

Did someone give you advice and point out to you the bad consequences of your choices in a certain direction, then you ignored it and it worked out exactly as they said? Do not wallow in regret. Pick your pieces and consider yourself a learner by experience and next time follow that advice when it is valid.

Did you take someone's advice and followed it immediately instead of thinking it through and regretted it because following it misled into a certain direction with dire consequences? Or did it happen because of your inclinations and lack of control?

Ultimately, most of the pain you hold inside is your responsibility. At times you might be discouraged by the chance of failure. Trying gives you the chance to win. You can see it through.

Chapter14: Improving Mental Strength

Living is an opportunity to train your mind to do the unimaginable. You have thought of ending it all because your mind is working well enough to reason and it just wants you to seek relief from pain.

Mind Power

If only you could realize how powerful your mind is, you would never want to die. Life is what you make it. You will always get what you focus on. Your mind drives your entire existence—thoughts, attitudes, perceptions, insight, knowledge, learning, and emotions. In short, you live in your mind. Your mind is your world. You have the ability to either make it a pleasant or unpleasant place.

Your mind controls your whole being. Therefore, it is important to form a good relationship with your mind. Imagine what happens when the power of an engine fails, it becomes impossible to move on. That is what a fatigued mind fed with disparaging thoughts does. Your mind can work in your favour if you control and train it to view life as important.

Practise controlling your thoughts. Your thoughts have the power to transform your life. You can unlearn a pattern of destructive thinking and start to think in constructive ways.

When you feed your mind with dark assessments of the world and others around you, negative self-conceptions of yourself or life in general, your mind will soon interpret the world as such. When you feed your mind with suicidal thoughts, soon enough you will engage in suicidal behaviour.

You train your mind through the information you feed it from external sources or your internal thoughts. Get rid of self-defeating thoughts.

Stop saying phrases like, "easier said than done" as a response to encouraging words. Just do life. If you win you will get satisfaction, and if you fail you will get a lesson for future use.

Look for solutions beyond your physical existence, when life seems unbearable. What happens to you affects you based on how you think and react.

Dwelling on sad thoughts worsens the situation. Dwelling on hopeful thoughts improves coping ability.

When your friend does something that hurts your feelings, you can choose to be angry or to forgive. Your friend does not make you angry. How you think about what your friend did makes you angry. If you decide to go to the bar and drink yourself to death, your friend did not make you drink, how you react is your own choice.

Your mind cannot be caged unless you choose to do so yourself. Your mind remains your own. It is your responsibility to polish and exercise its abilities for it to become stronger.

The important thing is to train your mind to consider things based on perspective rather than emotions. To lament is an easy option. Suicide might seem like a desirable way out of awful situations. However, to get on with living requires mental toughness.

Mental strength gives you the ability to overcome sadness, pain, disappointment and sorrow. Your mind requires more than intelligence. Intelligence as we know it does not give you the strength to tolerate losses and other uncomfortable situations.

Developing Mental Strength

Your mind is powerful, but it needs strengthening exercises. You develop mental strength by exercising your mind's ability to think, reason, create and solve problems. Human beings need mental toughness for survival and progress. You may lack physical strength, but your mental strength keeps you going.

Consider these scenarios.
Scenario 1
Players in a field do not go through with the game because of their strong physique only. Without mental strength, they would not be able to persevere tough training, focus on winning, be disciplined, or to respect their teammates.

Scenario 2
Have you heard about people on their death bed encouraging their loved ones even more than their loved ones encourage them? They have developed the mental toughness to face life and they have overcome the fear of death.

Scenario 3
One person will think of ending their life because of a seemingly small issue in their life, while others survive through terrifying circumstances and stand strong.

Mental toughness differs from one person to another, just as there are variations of physical toughness. Sometimes circumstances make other people develop mental strength earlier than others.

Between a person who does jobs which require physical strength and a person who requires minimum strength to work, whose muscles will be more developed?

You can work on your mental strength, grow it, and use it to improve the quality of your life. Just as physical strength, mental strength does not come easily or automatically.

You have to practice. Put in more effort and care. You have to train your mind to be tough.

Some of this training may be provided within your environment through circumstances you have no control over, while at times you may need to actively learn and develop mental toughness.

Tough times in life are the best trainers of mental toughness. You cannot be mentally strong without overcoming obstacles.

It is hard work. However, anyone who has a mind can develop mental toughness.

Signs that you are Mentally Strong

1. A mentally strong person is resilient.
Instead of avoiding tough times and strong negative emotions, you face them. You do not let hardships to distract you from your goals. You have strong willpower to cope through adversity. A personal set of coping mechanisms help you to go through life despite the challenges.

Adversity does not make you cower, instead, it is what motivates you to stand stronger knowing that if you made it through before, you will make it through again. Instead of "killing you, it makes you stronger." You persevere when you know there is enough gain eventually.

You are often being knocked hard by problems, but you retain your life. You perceive your challenges in life as opportunities to develop your mental strength.
2. A mentally strong person is disciplined.
Mental strength and discipline are birds of the same feather. Discipline requires the courage to keep moving on even when you no longer feel like doing so.

It involves the mental ability to choose one thing over the other, even if the other option seems easier than the right one.
Therefore, if you are disciplined, you have mental strength. The more you practice being disciplined the more you develop mental toughness.

3. A mentally strong person respects other people.

You understand that other people are also human beings blessed with the ability to reason, but you respect them for reasoning differently.

You are a good listener, and this makes you able to tolerate people who go against your views. You do not become angry when people disagree with you. However, you try to understand their perspective, even though you might not agree.

Hence, being mentally tough involves being capable of working with other people as part of a team despite your different backgrounds or ways of thinking. You can accommodate other people despite having different opinions.

4. A mentally strong person acts rather than reacts.

Instead of reacting to your emotions, you act most beneficially. You evaluate your choices. They are not based on emotions only. Since you have values that you stand for, you cannot react to everything.

Reacting threatens your core values. You have emotions as any other normal human being, but because of your mental toughness ability, your emotions do not control you. You control them.

5. A mentally strong person enjoys solitude.

A person with mental toughness has to be self-aware. You know your desires, interests, goals, personality, abilities, and limitations. You do not mind spending time in solitude so that you can examine yourself, meditate, and enjoy your own company. Other people are good company and you enjoy socializing, but you also enjoy your own company. You can be alone and comfortable.

6. A mentally strong person stands for something.

We all face moments of uncertainty when we hesitate to make decisions. But, as a mentally strong person, you have values that you stand for. Therefore, you are a decisive person. You do not decide to do things just because everyone else is doing them. You do what you do because you believe in it. You are assertive when necessary. Saying "no" is easy for you. You are not swayed by the crowd. You can think for yourself and make rational decisions. You stand firm for what you believe in.

7. A mentally strong person has a winning mindset.

You know what you want, you set goals to reach them, and you believe you will achieve them. You are hopeful for the best results.

And in case you lose, you do not wallow in hopelessness, instead, you take the loss as a learning experience.

You have strong hope and faith that all will be well as long as you keep working at winning. Hence, being mentally strong means being a good loser, but not giving up easily.

8. A mentally strong person is focused.

You focus on what you do and avoid distractions which may lead to confusion. You know what you want. When you set your mind to achieve it, then, you must achieve it.

Distinguishing between the most important things and the non-important things is second nature to you. You stick to your priorities. You do not lose your focus easily, even when under pressure to do so.

9. A mentally strong person is courageous.

You are fearless and you face life with optimism. You do not put yourself in danger cowardly. Nevertheless, you are not afraid to take great calculated risks which you know will bear fruit in the end. You make bold moves in your life without hesitating or being distracted by discouraging external influences.

10. A mentally strong person is persistent.

You know what you want and you seek to achieve it. Even when you fail at first, you keep trying. You try different methods of doing things rather than rigidly sticking to one.

When one way does not lead you to your destination, you create another and follow it.

You know what you want to achieve and for this reason, you work toward achieving it despite being bombarded with chaos which can make you feel like giving up.

Summary
Mental strength is developed through challenges. Therefore, look at your challenges in life as opportunities to develop your mental strength. Whenever you come out of hard times you will be stronger than you were before. If you give up, your strength will not develop.

Sometimes when life seems unbearable, try changing your perspective. Instead of viewing what you are going through as insurmountable, view it as a chance for you to develop your mental toughness.

Chapter15: Embracing Change

God grant me the serenity to accept the things I cannot change; courage to change the things I can; and wisdom to know the difference. ***Reinhold Niebuhr***

Life appears impossible to tolerate when you resist change. Human beings are always changing, thus, refusing to change causes duress. Change is often tough, isn't it? Especially when the change is negative and requires sacrificing some aspects of your life. Like from riches-to-rags changes.

You might assume only negative change is impossible to surpass. However, rags-to-riches changes can be tough too. Any change needs adjustment. Adjustments require effort. Hence, sometimes change is a daunting task. It is not strange to see somebody in a new status still doing things that he did before he got into the new place though those things are now considered unnecessary. When you do something for so long, it becomes part and parcel of you. Changing the established habit becomes a dire challenge, but it is not impossible.

In certain situations, there is no other alternative apart from choosing to change. Like in the unfortunate event that you lose your loved ones, fall ill, lose your job or marriage.

Or in the fortunate event that you experience a major improvement or success in your life like marriage, birth or a job promotion. In all these situations, failing to adapt to change can harm you mentally.

Changing is not as easy as saying "I've changed" or "I will change." Even being told to change is not enough to make you adapt to change. It is an inside job. A major change needs a complete shift in your mentality.

This involves changing your behaviour, attitudes, beliefs, habits, perception, thoughts and inclinations which are no longer serving you right.

Stages of Change

1. **Recognizing the need for change**

When situations crop up that require you to change, it is your recognition of the need for change that will motivate you to do so. For instance, when you marry no one needs to tell you to stop acting single, you need to recognize it is time to behave like a married person.

2. **Thinking about change**

After your awareness about the need for change, you start to contemplate the idea of changing.

This is a tough stage because you recognize the challenge of adapting to change. It requires strong reasoning to weigh which changes are necessary and which are not.

At this stage, you decide on the specific changes that you need to embrace. Changing could become a life or death matter. Often people commit suicide because they were unable to embrace circumstantial changes.

3. Planning for change

When you are contemplating about changing, plan how to embrace the change. What should you discard and what should you keep? What can help you to embrace the required changes?

4. Putting the plan into action

You can recognize the need for change, think about it and plan for change, but if you do not practice what you have planned the effort will be useless.

Let's say you are sent to work in another town and you need to move because of the distance. You recognize the need to move because travelling the distance will be costly and tiresome. Then you think about how changing will be beneficial, the challenges of looking for a house, and adapting to a new environment.

Next, you plan how to look for a house and how to move. Finally, you pack your stuff and move.

5. Continuing with the new actions

The last stage of change is embracing the change itself. It is often tough in the beginning. You will adapt to it provided that you do not wallow in thoughts of what could have been. You can make small adjustments until you can achieve the desired change.

The best way to adapt to change is to live in the present moment. After you adapt to change the ultimate step is to adopt the change into your daily life.

Learn from the Butterfly

Before it reaches optimum maturity, the butterfly goes through a lot of changes, and it adapts accordingly since it is necessary for its survival. It stops living the life of a crawling creature and begins to live the life of a flying creature. During the transformation, it closes itself up and isolates itself in preparation for the change.

What do you learn from the butterfly's metamorphosis? Sometimes life necessitates change, and you need to accept it even though the process is difficult.

Stop living the life of a crawling creature and begin to live the life of a flying creature.

Summary

Are you struggling to find out why you set achievable goals and yet you cannot seem to reach them? Are you in the pursuit of happiness and peace of mind?

Think about the behaviour, attitudes, beliefs, habits, perception, thoughts and inclinations that you need to change to achieve your goals. Do not let your inability to adapt to change block you from pursuing your goals or moving on from tough situations.

Chapter 16: Don't Quit on Yourself

You will experience days when you think of giving up. Plans will fail. Dreams will die. Losses will occur. People will quit on you. Make a pact with yourself not to be one of those people. In this chapter, I exhort you not to quit. Don't quit on yourself. Don't give up. Don't lose hope. Don't choose to stop living. Don't quit.

What's Pushing You to Quit?

Sometimes life will go in the wrong direction contrary to your anticipations. Things do not always go the way we plan them to. Sometimes our plans go well and life continues as we want it to, but sometimes things do not work out as planned.

Certainly, at some point in your life, you will face challenges or hard times. There are times when you will be overwhelmed in a given aspect of your life. Such negative feelings arise from unfulfilled desires and unmet needs. They thwart your ability to move on.

Issues like financial problems and marital conflict can lead to quitting. When you are in debt, you have no happiness because you know you are obligated to pay back. When you experience lack in an important area of your life and the inability to regain control, quitting looks like an appealing option.

Why Not Quit?

You might ask, why live when my life is unbearable, worthless and painful? Life is meant to be lived. Life is a natural gift bestowed upon you.

Also, it was meant for you to enjoy cheerfully and happily. Life itself is enjoyable and beautiful. The challenges you face in life cause pain and heartache. Some situations in life make life unbearable. All these miseries are against what you were created to do. Naturally, you may start to contemplate ending your life when your innate desires about it are not met.

You want to be happy. However, difficulties make it hard to achieve happiness. Your circumstances deny you happiness. Your life has so many low moments that you lack humour. You are rarely happy. You are often tired and disillusioned. Your mind is full of worry, frustration, uncertainty or anxiety brought about by the problems you undergo in life. Although you feel like you cannot go on, don't quit.

At a time when you are uncertain and you lack strength, you may perceive the aspired goal to be so far away. Yet, it could be nearer than you think. Don't let your current miserable situation to impair your judgment. You may be so near to where you want to be.

It is a great feeling to achieve the desired result after being a "struggler" for a while. Victory does not come easy. The best success comes after periods of struggling and not giving up. Don't quit because of the struggle.

When you quit you lose the chance of being victorious. When you quit, you lose. However, when you don't quit, you have a chance of winning.

You will regret it after you have quit due to fear of the struggle, but it will be too late to do anything about it. You will regret it when you realize that you were so close to achieving your anticipated goal, but then you gave up. Life is unpredictable but always hope for the best. You will likely never know exactly what will happen next. However, if you quit, you might regret it later.

Success and failure are closely related. Look at your failure as a learning opportunity. You can turn your failure into success. Success exists beneath failure and failure exists beneath success.

Your perceived success in life is the ultimate hope. Don't quit because of your doubts. Go ahead even when you are doubtful. You can acquire success. Success does not give you a due date. Have a flexible view of success because you cannot be completely sure of the exact time that you will achieve success.

You may think you are not going to succeed, yet you are very close to success. The opposite is true. You may think that you are close to success, yet you still have a long way to go. Be confident that you can have a successful life, but do not give room to pride and arrogance.

How Not to Quit

Life is a fight, and it will often present you with pain or hardships. You have been knocked out by many challenges in life and somehow you have survived. You can continue to live even when you face bigger challenges. You will only know what you can achieve in life if you stay alive.

When facing difficult circumstances that tire you, there is another option apart from quitting life. The option is to rest. Don't quit. Rest and get up to breathe another day's air. What happens when you are climbing a hill and you quit in the middle? All the effort you made to reach your current position will be a waste.

What if you rest a bit? Then, you can continue pursuing your goals in life after recuperation.

Always consider other options which do not involve quitting. Being overwhelmed signifies it is time to rest not time to quit.

You can achieve sought-after goals. Set goals that are achievable to you. In the pursuit of achievement, don't let obstacles keep you from achieving your dreams. You cannot wish hardships away.

What's the point of living in a state of, "I could have done it had it not been for some certain obstacles?" Live in a state of, "I am doing it despite these obstacles."

Obstacles might slow you down, but don't let them cause a premature stop. Most of these obstacles are a product of your pessimistic thinking patterns. When having suicidal thoughts, you are your worst enemy. Therefore, changing your way of thinking solves most of your problems.

As long as you keep going there is a chance for success. You can win. Giving up destroys that chance. Find out what you want to achieve in life and reach for it.

Give yourself another chance. You may succeed the next time you try again. It is not a guarantee that the next attempt will succeed, but how would you know if you can succeed if you give up?

Failures don't make quitting worthwhile. They show you that you should change what you are doing or how you are doing it.

It is a common occurrence to give up after struggling for some time because the situation seems hopeless. If one way fails, try another and another. Success does not come easy. You have to fight for it.

When Not to Quit

Embrace the unpredictability of life. It can feel strange, but it is not a new thing. Every human being learns this in the course of their life. Life does not always go smoothly. You will encounter changes in your life. Some changes are unexpected while others are expected.

What you expect you can prepare for. What you don't expect is harder to handle. Either way, this is normal in life. Don't quit, since life is like that. Take heart because it will not always be difficult.

After a failure, it is easier to give up than to move forward. Don't quit just because you have experienced failure. Your win might just be around the corner.

Don't give up when you fail once. Don't give up because failure has slowed you down. Keep moving. Beyond this bad result, there could be a good result. Many who have quit were just about to succeed. Don't quit on yourself when you feel like doing so.

Don't quit during what you consider to be the worst times. You can go through your hard situations. Things sometimes are not the worst, they just appear to be at their worst. You must not quit during hard times. Always fight against thoughts of quitting on yourself.

Chapter 17: Citing Reasons for Living

You are still here. That's a good reason for you to keep living. Many are dead and yet they loved life. Unfortunately, there is nothing like life transplantation. Otherwise, it would have been easy to simply exchange your life with someone else's who still wants to live and yet they are dying.

Nevertheless, that cannot be done. Well, it cannot be done yet, unless science finds a way to do it. Until then you have your life.

If you think you are useless, that is a limiting belief. Maybe you have not found out what you can do yet, but if you quit you will never know. Or maybe you must look more keenly. Pain can turn into experiences that lead you to your ultimate reason for living. The problem is we look at only one side of the pain when it is always two-faced.

Many people would do anything to stay alive, but they were denied this chance. Appreciate how privileged you are to be alive. Remember, you will always get what you focus on. Focus on living a decent life.

Reasons to quit

What are your reasons for wanting to die? The answer to this is the same as the answer to—

what reason do you have to continue living?

Write down your reasons for quitting life. Your reasons for quitting reveal the source of the problem. With them, you can derive an antithesis. As opposed to quitting, take alternative action to solve the problem.

For instance, if your reason for quitting is humiliation from others, the source of the problem is a negative emotion. Your reason to live can be to support others who are humiliated too.

Reasons to live

Write down your reasons for living. Your reasons for living reveal your priorities. Add to the list regularly when a reason to live strikes your mind. If possible. Write at least one sentence a day. Avoid placing a dot at the end of the sentence. Life goes on.

Here is a sample list citing reasons for living.

- I live because I have the capability to live

- I live because I can

- I am still here

- I refuse to end my own life because an enemy can end my life anytime

- I can achieve more when I am alive

- I have people I care about who I do not want to leave behind

• Some people care about me

• Worse people are alive and in hiding to keep alive, and I am a fairly good person

• In a crowd of 7 billion, I occupy my own unique space

• I am part of the atoms that make up the universe

• I celebrate life—the joy of the act of living itself

• I accept suffering is part of life, it is unavoidable, in one way or the other I will suffer

• I enjoy my state of being and my fleeting presence

• Life is a learning experience and I have so much to learn

• God made me with the reason and purpose to live the life He has given me

• I like sharing happy moments with significant others

• I hope to inspire someone's life through my life, words and actions

• I love to contribute something to the world

- If I quit I will never know the extent of my endurance and other inborn human possibilities
- I have found meaning and purpose for my pain
- People have quit on me, and I do not want to join them
- The only person who cannot quit on me is myself
- I know most pain is borne by my thoughts and I do not want to lose the battle against my self-destructive thinking
- However bad it is and however much I do not want to see it, there are always two or more ways by which I can regard the situation
- I am superior in a unique way since I know my kind of pain more than someone else
- I can help and encourage others who are in the same situation as mine to get out of it only by getting out of it rather than quitting

- I respect myself and my life despite my mistakes

- I have a higher purpose in life than mere existence

- I enjoy breathing in and out, sleeping and waking up

- I just have one thing to do and I choose to do it right—my life

- I am learning to love my life as it is instead of running from life wishing it was not like this (Who knows if in alternative life I would have the same problems or worse?)

- I get angry with life because some things in life are a threat to my happiness, but I will not let my emotions be a threat to my life

- I was given my life, thus I am the owner and not a victim of my life

- I am determined not to quit since my problems and some people are determined to make me quit

- I can achieve the success I want, but I cannot get it if I quit

• I do not want to quit when I tell myself that I want to quit even though sometimes I do not realize it

• I am an ordinary human being so I have weaknesses. I am a unique human being I own my strengths

• Society does not know me like God knows me and like I know myself

• I own my failures and successes in the same measure

• No emotion lasts forever, neither the bad ones nor the good ones

• Thinking about what I can cause to happen instead of thinking only about what happens to me gives me the joy of living

• I have the courage and the wisdom needed to survive on Earth

Chapter 18: 100 Upsetting Realities of Life

In the previous chapters, this book mentions the importance of letting go of what you cannot control and accepting life changes. To jog your memory in case you are stuck in identifying such realities of life that might require accepting, here is my subjective list of upsetting realities of life. Read through then make your list of ugly truths. After which, note that those are the things in your life which require "accepting what you cannot change."

100 upsetting realities of life

1. You are dying.

2. You lose loved ones through death.

3. Loved ones make mistakes, they are not perfect.

4. Some people hurt you and behave as victims.

5. You break your own heart with negative attitudes and thoughts.

6. You have to let go of some people despite loving them.

7. People you trust and love are keeping secrets from you.

8.   You are keeping a secret (or secrets) from people you love.

9.   Some close friends will betray you.

10.   You will fail at something in life.

11.   You will encounter illness or the illness of your loved one.

12.   People will easily notice your small mistakes, but not your immense suffering.

13.   Everyone will not love you and you will not love everyone.

14.   Some things take time and you have to wait patiently.

15.   You can quickly lose everything you think you cannot live without.

16.   Sometimes you have to leave good things to gain better things.

17.   People will ignore you when they think they are better than you.

18.   Some people you think are your friends are not happy about your success and they can easily leave you for dead.

19.   Your friends, family and society will not always approve of your choices.

20. Some significant others will leave you when you are in trouble and appear when things seem good.

21. You will lend money to your friends and they will not pay it back.

22. Some people will hurt you and not see the gravity of their mistake even when tables turn and someone does to them exactly what they did to you.

23. At times you must apologize for being wrong and at times you must apologize even though you are right.

24. People will try to use you, manipulate you and lie to you.

25. You cannot avoid all bad situations in life.

26. Success requires sacrificing time, relationships and other goals.

27. Being a good person is not a guarantee for visible success and prowess.

28. Some evil people do well, and some good people suffer.

29. The greater the success the bigger the fear of failure.

30.   Material things will never satisfy you unless you have inner peace.

31.   You can never please everybody and everybody cannot please you.

32.   You are equal to other human beings by virtue of being.

33.   Other people will hate you because of how other people love you.

34.   Some people will praise you in your face, but harshly criticise you behind your back.

35.   When you constantly think negatively you cannot attain happiness.

36.   How you look on the outside matters.

37.   Some people are kind to you; not because they care, but because it makes them feel better, gives them validation, and personal fulfilment.

38.   You will feel like you are not good enough at something.

39.   You will always meet someone better or worse than you.

40. You cannot know everything in a lifetime.

41.   You cannot escape old age as long as you are alive.

42.   Some people will help you, not because they love you, but because you are their self-esteem booster.

43.   People will use you, you will use people and life goes on.

44.   You will do things which are not good for you at some point in life.

45.   The unexpected will always happen to ruin your plans.

46.   Things are not always as they seem neither are people, neither are you.

47.   You will break some hearts and your heart will be broken.

48.   You cannot be friends with everyone.

49.   Enemies motivate you more than friends.

50.   The world is wicked and there is nothing you can do about it.

51.   Your life can take a drastic turn for the better or the worst anytime.

52.   We all have 24 hours in a day.

53. The longer you live, the more the people you lose.

54. Everybody lies.

55. No positive or negative emotion lasts forever.

56. Society will pressure you to conform, and no matter how hard you try at some point you will.

57. Social media life and real life are two different things.

58. At some point in your life, you will be a victim of a situation you never imagined yourself in.

59. Sometimes you will see your loved one suffering helplessly and there is nothing you can do about it.

60. You will face some type of societal injustice in your lifetime.

61. Sometimes you will be so sure that you are right, but it will turn out you were wrong.

62. You will be so sure you are wrong, but it will turn out you were right.

63. Most people will not understand you and neither will you understand most people.

64. You can be a criminal or a victim of crime anytime.

65. You will witness an accident, be in an accident or cause an accident.

66. It is difficult to admit your own mistakes but you will see other people's mistakes easily.

67. It is easier to believe bad news than good news and bad things about others than good things.

68. You cannot be an optimist all the time.

69. Many people just dream of having a life like yours.

70. If you live to please people, or impress people you will never be free.

71. You live alone most of the time.

72. Trying to control what is beyond your control causes needless suffering.

73. You see things as you are, and it takes a lot of practice to see things as they are.

74. Do not get too attached to your position in your friend's life, it will constantly change.

75.   You have judged people wrongly and you have been judged wrongly by people.

76.   Sometimes the bad things people say about you are true.

77.   You can never know for sure whether the person who says they love you truly loves you.

78.   Life is tough for everyone at some point, even when you are rich.

79.   You cannot change the past.

80.   You cannot undo sensing something. You cannot "un-see," "un-hear," "un-touch" etc. once it is done.

81.   Life changes and you can roll with it or get stuck and suffer.

82.   Life is fragile. You might not be here tomorrow.

83.   You will have to depend on people to do things for you at some point in life.

84.   Sometimes you must trust a stranger.

85.   Life is hard and cruel.

86.   You will be coned and manipulated at some point, no matter how clever you are.

87.   You cannot control how other people think of you, that is their choice.

88.   That person you are willing to die for, might not be willing to do the same for you.

89.   People do not think or talk about you as much as you think they do.

90.   You are spending your time worrying over trivial issues which will not matter in a few years to come.

91.   You realize the importance of people during their absence.

92.   Talking and complaining about someone or something does not fix the problem.

93.   An empty life cannot be filled with money or material things.

94.   Someone thinks you are a bad person.

95.   Sometimes people you love need some time away from you.

96.   You can never have the same experience twice.

97.   Sometimes your role in a romantic relationship is to build your partner for his/her future spouse.

98. Solitary time for meditation and reflection is important for personal growth.

99. You only need food, clothing, and shelter to be happy, the rest is an illusion.

100. We might or might not be alone in the universe.

Chapter 19: Citing Moments of Happiness

It seems impossible to find joy for living when your mental pain challenges your being. Activities which you have always considered to be fun lose their meaning. Your enthusiasm for doing anything goes beyond negative 1000. With time you lose interest in life itself.

The past is not always a bad thing, you can learn from it. Most times we refer to the bad things when talking about forgetting the past. Now, let's remember the past a bit, but let's bring it to the present.

For this list, write using the present tense. Create a list of your happy moments, ranging between tiny and enormous.

Label it "my moments of happiness." List as many as possible and describe your moments more whenever possible. Address yourself using the word "you." Remember to be very honest with yourself.

Note that if you quit life, you will deny yourself the chance to enjoy such moments or the memory of such moments.

Continue adding to the list daily. Add something that pleases you even for a second.

Look at my list below as a sample. I intentionally left out the full stops at the end to symbolize my hope for more moments.

My moments of happiness

1. When you wake up in the morning and you feel refreshed.

2. When you go to sleep early after a tiresome day

3. When you go to bed straight after taking a shower

4. When children open up their arms wide wanting you to carry them

5. When someone you like tells you they like you or they do something nice for you

6. When you sit next to someone you love

7. When you are thinking about someone, you reach for your phone to call or text them and your phone rings. It is either a text or a call from them

8. When you are served a delicious meal that you did not participate in preparing

9. When you have the freedom to serve yourself food

10.   When you see people you love enjoying a meal that you prepared for them

11.   When you sit somewhere and your phone detects free Wi-Fi. When the free Wi-Fi does not have a password

12.   When you are told that a certain plan has been cancelled after your motivation to go had reduced, and you were trying to come up with an excuse

13.   When you receive a surprise gift from someone you love. When you are buying a gift for someone

14.   When you receive a real hug that is more than merely putting the head on this side and then the other. The hug comes from a family member, friend or someone else you adore

15.   When your child beats even the simplest of growth milestones. When your baby smiles, struggles to sit, makes cooing sounds, calls you by name, says your full names, says the first word, ask a funny question, stands for the first time, takes a step in your presence and starts to reason

16.   When your child is carried up by someone and looks around for you in a crowd of people then comes to you

17.   When you are on stage and people cheer you before you even start performing. When you give a speech or a talk that you had not prepared for and people commend you

18.   When you hear that a notorious criminal has been given the life sentence. Better when you hear that the person has died

19.   When you succeed in chasing away a wasp that had entered your house

20.   When a beautiful bird enters your house

21.   When you sit down with snacks and a cup of tea, coffee or a refreshing drink just relaxing

22.   When you watch a movie, with outstanding acting, a comedy, epic romance, or you read or hear a story whereby the villain loses

23.   When travelling and you encounter beautiful scenery, perhaps a lush green terrain, the view of a lake, flowers, or wild

animals. When you see a plantation such as of tea, sugarcane, sunflower from above

24. When you lie on the ground looking at a clear blue sky

25. When you finish a task or project

26. When you are given a compliment by someone you like or someone you admire. When your crush gives you attention despite having many options of people to show attention to

27. When you clear all loans you owe

28. When you receive money that you did not expect without working for it

29. When you experience a win after various failed attempts. When you are one of the candidates in the shortlist of a competition or a job opportunity

30. When you arrive late for work and your boss is not in yet

31. When you are served quickly. When you go to the bank and there is no queue. The teller serves you immediately and you don't have to wait for anything

32.   When you are hungry and someone offers you food without asking them to. When you are invited for lunch or dinner and you had no plans

33.   When you fall asleep and someone covers you with a clean sheet or duvet

34.   When you survive a near-death experience after you had lost hope.

35.   When you are being attacked and you hear police sirens and your attacker flees

36.   When you are in hospital and your significant others come with homemade food

37.   The moment the doctor tells you are discharged from hospital

38.   When you get a ride in a car that you cannot afford in your wildest dreams

39.   When you see someone interrupting a fight between two people and there is peace

40.   When there is a deep silence after a lot of noise in the environment

41.   When the moonlight shines through your curtains

42. When you look at the stars on a clear night with the naked eye. When you see a shooting star

43. When it rains after a long period of dry weather. It starts raining before you reach the house or the destination, you take cover, after a while, it stops raining. When the sun shines after the rain. When it rains and you are in the comfort of your bed

44. When you sleep under freshly cleaned beddings

45. When you drink a glass of water after a long period of thirst, or when you eat after a long time without food

46. When the power returns after a blackout. After a few days of the taps running dry, you hear the sound of water flowing from the taps

47. When you hear music and identify with the lyrics. When you hear music and you feel like dancing or singing

48. When a friend calls you to ask for advice.

49. When a friend trusts you enough to reveal to you some detail about their life without asking

50. When your prayer is answered in the most unexpected way at the most unexpected time after a long time. When Jehovah says "yes" after a long period of thinking that the answer was "no"

References

Barzilay, S., & Apter, A. (2014). Psychological models of suicide. *Archives of suicide research*, *18*(4), 295-312.

Campos, R. C., Holden, R. R., & Santos, S. (2018). Exposure to suicide in the family: Suicide risk and psychache in individuals who have lost a family member by suicide. *Journal of clinical psychology*, *74*(3), 407-417.

Cheavens, J. S., Cukrowicz, K. C., Hansen, R., & Mitchell, S. M. (2016). Incorporating resilience factors into the interpersonal theory of suicide: The role of hope and self-forgiveness in an older adult sample. *Journal of clinical psychology*, *72*(1), 58-69.

Hagan, C. R., Podlogar, M. C., Chu, C., & Joiner, T. E. (2015). Testing the interpersonal theory of suicide: The moderating role of hopelessness. *International Journal of Cognitive Therapy*, *8*(2), 99-113.

Hooley, J. M., Franklin, J. C., & Nock, M. K. (2014). Chronic pain and suicide: understanding the association. *Current pain and headache reports, 18*(8), 435.

Joiner, T. E., Ribeiro, J. D., & Silva, C. (2012). Nonsuicidal self-injury, suicidal behaviour, and their co-occurrence as viewed through the lens of the interpersonal theory of suicide. *Current Directions in Psychological Science, 21*(5), 342-347.

Kyaga, S., Landén, M., Boman, M., Hultman, C. M., Långström, N., & Lichtenstein, P. (2013). Mental illness, suicide and creativity: 40-year prospective total population study. *Journal of psychiatric research, 47*(1), 83-90.

Klonsky, E. D., & May, A. M. (2015). The three-step theory (3ST): A new theory of suicide rooted in the "ideation-to-action" framework. *International Journal of Cognitive Therapy, 8*(2), 114-129.

Lester, D., & Gunn, J. F. (2012). Perceived burdensomeness and thwarted belonging: An investigation of the interpersonal theory of suicide. *Clinical Neuropsychiatry, 9*(6), 221-224.

Phillips, M. R. (2010). Rethinking the role of mental illness in suicide.

Pompili, M. (2010). Exploring the phenomenology of suicide. *Suicide and Life-Threatening Behavior, 40*(3), 234-244.

Smith, P. N., & Cukrowicz, K. C. (2010). Capable of suicide: A functional model of the acquired capability component of the interpersonal-psychological theory of suicide. *Suicide and Life-Threatening Behavior, 40*(3), 266-275.

Steiner, G. A. (2010). *Strategic planning*. Simon and Schuster.

Troister, T., & Holden, R. R. (2010). Comparing psychache, depression, and hopelessness in their associations with suicidality: A test of Shneidman's theory of suicide. *Personality and Individual Differences, 49*(7), 689-693.

Troister, T., & Holden, R. R. (2013). Factorial differentiation among depression, hopelessness, and psychache in statistically predicting suicidality. *Measurement and evaluation in counseling and development, 46*(1), 50-63.

Turecki, G., & Brent, D. A. (2016). Suicide and suicidal behaviour. *The Lancet, 387*(10024), 1227-1239.

Van Orden, K. A. (2015). The interpersonal theory of suicide: A useful theory. *Psychology of emotions, motivations and actions. Advancing the science of suicidal behavior: Understanding and intervention,* 41-52.

Van Orden, K. A., Witte, T. K., Cukrowicz, K. C., Braithwaite, S. R., Selby, E. A., & Joiner Jr, T. E. (2010). The interpersonal theory of suicide. *Psychological Review, 117*(2), 575.

Verrocchio, M. C., Carrozzino, D., Marchetti, D., Andreasson, K., Fulcheri, M., & Bech, P. (2016).

Mental pain and suicide: a systematic review of the literature. *Frontiers in Psychiatry, 7*, 108.

Wang, Y., & Chiew, V. (2010). On the cognitive process of human problem-solving. *Cognitive systems research, 11*(1), 81-92.

World Health Organization Suicide Fact sheet. Updated September 2019. Retrieved from http://www.who.int/mediacentre/factsheets/fs398/en/.

Appendix I: Self-assuring Statements

Use these affirmations for comfort and assurance. Be tougher when the going gets tough:

- Now that I am not dead yet, I have the capability for survival
- I am built with the capability to tolerate, to persevere and to endure
- The capability for life is already in me
- I can overcome temporary and permanent losses and triumph over the disappointments, suffering and pain that I experience in this world
- I am still alive because I have the capability to live
- My inborn capability to live is not shrouded by the challenges I go through
- I regain my capability for life by willing myself to live despite the challenges I encounter
- I must take steps that will help me to increase my capability to do life

• I am reminding my mind of my inborn capability to live

• I live because I have the capability to live, thus, I live because I can.

• I belong to myself

• I belong to humanity

• I belong to life

• Hardships nurture my strength of spirit and mind

• Living is an opportunity to train my mind to do the unimaginable

• I know what I want and when I set my mind to achieve it, then, I must achieve

• I need to quit toxic habits, situations and people in my life that threaten my peace of mind

• My mind remains my own

• I train my mind to consider things based on perspective instead of emotions

• I am not a prisoner of a fixed negative mindset

• No matter where I am, I can influence someone's life positively

- No matter what happens to me, I can survive through my effort rather than die through my effort

- I will always find something to be grateful for, no matter how small it may seem

- I will become tougher when I get through tough times

- I made it through before, and I will make it through again

- I am at peace with myself

- I am at peace with being criticised and misunderstood

- I am at peace with my scars

- I am courageous and strong

- I am willing to accept assistance from the right places

- I am honest with myself

- I am ready to face the consequences of my actions

- I am grateful for my life

Appendix II: 50 Quotes on Quitting and Giving up

On Mistakes and Quitting

1. "Keep going. No matter what you do, no matter how many times you screw up and think to yourself "there's no point to carry on", no matter how many people tell you that you can't do it - keep going. Don't quit. Don't quit because a month from now you will be that much closer to your goal than you are now."—*Anonymous*

2. "If you live long enough, you'll make mistakes. But if you learn from them, you'll be a better person. It's how you handle adversity, not how it affects you. The main thing is never quit, never quit, never quit."—*Bill Clinton*

3. "Each mistake teaches you something new about yourself. There is no failure, remember, except in no longer trying. It is the courage to continue that counts."
—*Chris Bradford*

4.   "Success seems to be connected with action. Successful people keep moving. They make mistakes, but they don't quit."—*Conrad Hilton*

On Failure and Quitting

5.   "Failing is not the worst thing in the world; quitting is." —*Edwin Louis Cole*

6.   "One of the most common causes of failure is the habit of quitting when one is overtaken by temporary defeat." —*Napoleon Hill*

7.   "To quit is to fail - as long as you are still in the game you are succeeding!" —*Lindsey Rietzsch*

8.   "The easiest mistake to make is to lose sight of your goal. Failure is temporary, but quitting is permanent. Choose wisely."—*Kevin J. Donaldson*

9.   "If you're feeling discouraged and defeated—don't quit. Play on, hope on and move forward. The music you play—even in the midst of incredible darkness—can and

will turn the tide of your own battles."—*Seth Adam Smith*

10. "Never quit on your dream, but learn to cut your losses and quit your plan if it is not working."—*Ken Poirot*

11. "Having down moments doesn't make someone weak, it makes them human. We wouldn't be human if we don't "feel", but at some point, we must force ourselves to get up!"—*Yvonne Pierre*

On Tiredness and Quitting

12. "If you get tired, learn to rest, not to quit." —*Banksy*

13. "Run when you can, walk if you have to, crawl if you must; just never give up."—*Dean Karnazes*

14. "Awake! There is always a reason to give up and there is always a reason to soldier on unrelentingly. Don't give up so easily on a true purpose just because you perceive an arduous errand. Arise for you can do something to overcome something!"—*Ernest Agyemang Yeboah*

15. "Losers quit when they're tired. Winners quit when they've won."—*Mike Ditka*

On Success and Quitting

16. "Don't quit. Suffer now and live the rest of your life as a champion." —*Muhammad Ali*

17. "If you don't give up on something you truly believe in, you will find a way."—*Roy T. Bennet*

18. "There are tomorrows on their way worth the struggles of today. Never give up." —*Richelle E. Goodrich*

19. "Striving for successful goals will have a tendency at times to be discouraging, thankless, and mentally draining. You are entitled to these feelings, however, you are not entitled to give up."—*Dewayne Owens*

20. "You would never know what you are truly capable of until quitting is no longer a way out."—*Edmond Mbiaka*

21. "If you don't give up your hopes and dreams, then there will always be a good ending."—*Choi Minho*

22. "Never quit believing that you can develop in life. Never give up. Don't deny the inward spirit that provides the drive to accomplish great things in life." —*Jon Huntsman Sr.*

23. "Never quit. It is the easiest cop-out in the world. Set a goal and don't quit until you attain it. When you do attain it, set another goal, and don't quit until you reach it. Never quit."—*Bear Bryant*

On Thoughts and Quitting

24. "Quitting is not the answer. Life is not fair, and you can't quit every time something unfair happens to you."—*John Grisham*

25. "When your own mind tells you to quit, you must ignore your negative thoughts and press on."—*Robert Kiyosaki*

26. "There is definitely more left in you than what those negative thoughts are forcing you to believe. Quitting on yourself should

never be an option in your life. Success is your true destiny Keep pushing until something very rewarding happens."—*Edmond Mbiaka*

27. "Quitting is never an option on the road to success. Find the way forward. If you have a positive mindset and are willing to persevere, there is little that is beyond your reach. The attitude of being ready to work even in the face of challenges and despite odds is what will make all the difference in your life."—*Roopleen*

On Struggles and Quitting

28. "Never Quit...Never ever Quit...You might feel weak when there is someone stronger and more skilled than you are, but if you don't quit there is a chance to prove your determination...but quitting makes you lose already."—*Swetha Dhanagari*

29. "Even the best of us can falter in the face of an insurmountable task. But that does not mean we accept defeat."—*Saim .A. Cheeda*

30. "Never give up. Things may be hard, but if you quit trying they'll never get better. Stop worrying and start trusting God. It will be worth it."—*Germany Kent*

31. "Most people quit because they look how far they have to go, not how far they have come."—*Ziad K. Abdelnour*

32. "Stick to the fight when you're hardest hit–It's when things seem worst that you must not quit."—*Edgar A. Guest*

33. "Darkness should never be an excuse to quit, for, with God, darkness is the exact stuff that light was built for."—*Craig D. Lounsbrough*

34. "Fight if you must, work hard, give your best but never quit in the face of difficulty."—*Sanchita Pandey*

35. "There is much more joy in being a survivor than being a quitter."—*Omoakhuana Anthonia*

36. "Be aware that there can be tough moments when you're ready to throw in the towel. Frustrating times when you may want to quit. When it gets rough or you hit a

roadblock, you must forge ahead and keep going. Despite blood, sweat, and tears, do not give up on yourself. You are worth the fight for a brighter future!"—*Dana Arcur*

37.   "Pain is temporary. It may last a minute, or an hour, or a day, or a year, but eventually it will subside and something else will take its place. If I quit, however, it lasts forever. That surrender, even the smallest act of giving up, stays with me. So when I feel like quitting, I ask myself, which would I rather live with?"—*Lance Armstrong*

On Fear and Quitting

38. "If you're planning on quitting, first make sure it's not for one of these reasons:
Fear, Discomfort, Anger, Self-pity, Someone's negative opinions, Past failures, Unrealistic expectations."—*Charles F.Glassma*

39. "Without being pushed to the wall, we will have remained in our comfort zone. But this circumstance challenges us to find the courage to move on."—*Lailah Gifty Akita*

40. "Don't give up the search for happiness because you are afraid of getting hurt."—*Martha Raye*

One-liners

41. "Nothing's over 'til you quit."—*Alisha Rai*

42. "It's always too soon to quit!"—*Norman Vincent Peale*

43. "I never said it would be easy. Giving up is easy."—*Maria V. Snyder*

44. "Things can always get worse, but only quitters quit!"—*Nina Sakura*

45. "NEVER quit, quitting is NOT an option."—*Bob Proctor*

46. "If you quit once it becomes a habit. Never quit!"—*Michael Jordan*

47. "Champions don't quit."—*Mike Tyson*

48. "Winners never quit and quitters never win."—*Vince Lombardi*

49. "Quitting: easy. Daring to triumph: hard." —*Laird Hamilton*

50. "How am I to know what I can achieve if I quit?" —*Jason Bishop*

Notes

Notes

Epilogue

Thanks for reading this book. I might not identify with your current psychological pain as it is at the moment.

However, I do know how hard it can be to ask for advice or help. It is often tough to reach out for help, especially after you have tried to do so and it backfires. Sometimes instead of the problem being halved, sharing multiplies it. The reason could be: sharing with the wrong people; oversharing in one sitting; sharing when unprepared or human imperfection.

Let me tell you a bit about one of the difficult periods in my life and what helps me to overcome. Maybe by sharing this, I have revealed to the world my weak spots, my worries, my insecurities and whatnot. I will probably lose friends for this.

After a very painful experience in my life in which I was a victim of a heinous crime, I sought justice and it proved elusive. I confided in people and they blew up the matter by advertising my ordeal to others.

Strangers who did not know me and people I knew took my problems lightly and blamed me for a crime that was committed against me. I received a lot of well-meaning advice, which was more hurtful than silence because it revealed how people did not understand.

Some of my so-called friends mocked my pain and claimed that I was telling an imaginary story. Some pretended to listen only to betray me later. I always found out because I am a private person. It takes a lot of courage for me to open up. When I share something with someone in confidence, I have likely shared with that individual only. So, after the rumours spread and my issues retold to me in another version (with a bit of truth and a lot of distortion) by another person, I could know the source.

Besides the trauma of what I had been through, no one seemed to understand and things were getting worse. I regretted opening up. I felt weak, powerless, and scattered. It was like the entire world was against me. However, in reality, it was not.

Support

Not all friends, relatives, and strangers were inconsiderate. My immediate family members were supportive, although most of the time they did not know what to do, being present was enough.

An acquaintance once complimented me for my resilience. I believed I was strong because my circumstances were pathetic and somehow I was managing. But resilient? No, I had not thought about that. I started to see myself as resilient and now I know that I am.

Two of my friends rarely said a word, but they would frequently invite me to their place for a meal or tea.

They would quote scriptures and assure me of their support without giving unsolicited advice or harshly criticising me. They made me feel loved and this was therapeutic.

I did not go for therapy immediately because I was unemployed and paying for therapy would have overstretched my wallet.

When I did, the counsellor listened and assured me of confidentiality as long as he had no reason to believe that I could harm myself or another. He did not give me useless advice. He did not tell me to stop crying and he did not jump into conclusions quickly. The mental health professional helped me through my cognitive distortions and I viewed life differently.

After termination of the counselling, he followed up with me, sent seasonal greetings and gave practical suggestions for where I could get jobs. For some reason, he thought money would solve 50% of my stress. He was right.

Lessons

I learnt great lessons during those difficult times. Some of them as follows:

I learnt who the real people in my life are, the ones who support you even when you are hard to support.

I identified people to cut off from my life. Those in my circle who would rather bring me down than uplift me.

They would shower me with praises of how I was a strong woman, give unsolicited advice, and exhort me to talk to them about my plight. However, as soon as I left, they would tear me down and laugh at me.

Some seek to know how you are doing just to console themselves by weighing how much better they are and look for material for the next hot discussion they will have about you.

It is important to understand that whether people have some genetic relationships, whether they have lived longer than you, whether they have a PhD in Psychiatry, as long as they have not been through what you have been through, they are likely to lack the ability to put themselves in your shoe.

Your shoe is too pathetic for them to try on. They are glad when bad things happen to you because it makes them feel better about themselves.

Coping

I had a death wish, but a desire to procreate kept me going. I realise now that, subconsciously, I did not want to die before leaving traces of my DNA on this planet. I hope you can find your own motivation to keep going.

My immediate family members and real friends stood beside me when the world was against me, though I had let them down. If you have a supportive family that cares about you deeply and are always there for you, cherish, appreciate, and value them. If not, that is no reason to give up, because you can create your own. Family is not always about blood ties.

My faith in Jehovah's mercy and forgiveness kept me going. In the end, it does not matter what human beings do to me, think of me or say about me, all that matters is what God sees when he looks at my heart.

God's love for you does not depend on human beings' opinions. No matter what people say about you, or do to you, they are not powerful enough to block God's blessings, forgiveness, and love from your life.

In a more recent traumatic experience, on 11th March 2019, an angry mob attacked us while on duty at a village together with three other colleagues.

In our work as probation officers, we interact with both offenders and victims of crime. We often encounter hostile people, but never to the extent of that particular day.

The mob was out for blood and they almost killed us. We had already explained to them who we are and our reason for the visit. But the owner of the home we had visited to conduct the social inquiry, incited the villagers. They stopped listening. We begged for our lives, but they would not listen. We knew we were going to die for nothing.

The noise of the mob enveloped our cries. We were marooned and tied with ropes to ensure we would not escape.

People who did not know us, people stronger than us, but looking at us with murder in their eyes and unleashing their whips, blows, and stones while aiming for our heads.
As they beat us up, it seemed they believed they were doing a great service to God. They believed they were getting justice. Yet, we were mere strangers doing our job and had nothing to do with their predicament.

It was that kind of situation where the only thing left to do is pray. We owe our lives to God and the people He sent to rescue us.

I had been working on this book and postponing, but I suddenly came face to face with the reminder that life is delicate, people are wicked, anything can happen, others can kill me, and I did not want to die before finishing this project.
I also learned that some concerns I had in earlier ordeals (e.g. being misunderstood and gossiped about as narrated above) were useless trivialities. I would rather be backstabbed figuratively than backstabbed factually.

We are still dealing with the aftermath of that unjust experience, but by now most people who sympathised with us have forgotten about it. It is normal.

Some of our colleagues (people we would expect to understand the risks of our job) mocked us for almost being lynched to death.

Some were insensitive with their comments and took photos of our gruesome injuries and posted them online without our consent. However, some are kind, understanding, helpful, and patient with us.

I am still trying to make my peace with that experience and its aftermath. To date, I panic when in crowds, when I hear people shouting, and I cannot handle certain cases.

Sometimes, it gets overwhelming and I desire to "rest in peace."

Nonetheless, that story deserves a book of its own.

Life is hard, life is precious and life is fragile for all of us.

Let's keep moving forward. We did not give up. We are not giving up. We will not give up. Suicide is not the only solution to life's problems.

Life is for living. Keep living. Don't give up. Don't quit. Do life.

S.C

About the Author

Sophy Chunge lives in Kenya. Her interests include; psychology, humanity, poetry, art, music, reading, editing, writing, travelling and preaching the Good News. She advocates for mental health within the community and through her writing. *The Big Dilemma* is her non-fiction debut. Visit her website at **https://www.centfie.com**

www.ingramcontent.com/pod-product-compliance
Lightning Source LLC
Chambersburg PA
CBHW050339160726
48002CB00001B/376